OF LAW AND LIFE & OTHER THINGS THAT MATTER

PAPERS AND ADDRESSES OF

Felix Frankfurter

1956–1963

Harris & Ewing

OF LAW AND LIFE & OTHER THINGS THAT MATTER

PAPERS AND ADDRESSES OF

Felix Frankfurter

1956–1963

EDITED BY PHILIP B. KURLAND

ORIGINALLY PUBLISHED BY THE BELKNAP PRESS OF
HARVARD UNIVERSITY PRESS

ATHENEUM 1969 NEW YORK

Published by Atheneum
Reprinted by arrangement with Harvard University Press

Library of Congress Catalog Card Number 65-7916
Manufactured in the United States of America by
The Murray Printing Company
Forge Village, Massachusetts
Published in Canada by McClelland and Stewart Ltd.
First Atheneum Edition

PREFATORY NOTE

I AM indebted with affectionate gratitude to my learned friend, Professor Philip B. Kurland, of The Law School, The University of Chicago, for collecting the fugitive pieces herein and giving them permanence by putting them between the covers of a book. Nor can I fail to express my warm appreciation to my wife for improvingly editing some of these pieces in their original form by means of her skillful pen and literary taste.

Felix Frankfurter

Washington, D. C.
August 5, 1964

CONTENTS

OF LAW AND LIFE & OTHER THINGS THAT MATTER

«I»

Postscript to M'Naghten's Case

The following exchange of letters took place between Mr. Justice Frankfurter and Sir William Haley of *The Times* (London) after *The Times* referred to *M'Naghten's Case* as *M'Naughten's Case*. The correspondence was first published in *The Law Quarterly Review* 74:321 (January 1958).

SUPREME COURT OF THE UNITED STATES

Washington, D.C.
November 3, 1952

Dear Sir William:

That poor creature, Daniel M'Naghten, not only killed an innocent man, but also occasioned considerable conflict between law and medicine. But in so doing he gave his name to a leading case and thus obtained a permanent place in the history of the law. I am sure that *The Times* does not want to make inroads on his fame. A strange fatality has dogged the spelling of his name; too often it is incorrectly spelled. It is M'Naghten, not M'Naughten or any of the variants of its misspelling.

Or am I wrong in relying on the spelling given by Clark and Finnelly in their report of the case? See *Daniel M'Naghten's Case*, 10 Cl. & Fin. 200.

Sincerely yours,
Felix Frankfurter

Sir William J. Haley

THE TIMES

November 10, 1952

Dear Mr. Justice Frankfurter:

The strong leaven of Daniel M'Naghten still works on. He is a benefactor indeed to have occasioned a letter from you. The interesting thing about the point you raise is that all through the proof stages of the article M'Naghten had appeared as such, but so strong is the tradition of *The Times* that it altered to M'Naughten just as it was going to press. One of the most powerful things which hits a newcomer to Printing House Square is the magnificent strength of tradition, and the fact is that that was how *The Times* spelt him in its report of the original trial.

The exact spelling has been a problem down the years. No doubt high authority must be given to Clark and Finnelly but there are other authorities, dare I say it, equally high who disagree. It may amuse you to have the following short list got out by the writer of the article when I told him you had raised the point. (Incidentally, he is that kind of man.)

1. The original Gaelic—Mhicneachdain
2. The lunatic himself, signing a letter produced at the trial —M'Naughten (as reported in *The Times*).
3. The State Trials—Macnaughton
4. Clark and Finnelly—M'Naghten
5. Archbold, 1938 edition—Macnaughton
1927 edition—Macnaughten
Index—Macnaghten
6. Stephen, earlier editions—Macnaughten
later editions—Macnaghten
7. Halsbury, earlier editions—M'Naughton
later editions—M'Naughten
8. Select Committee on Capital Punishment, 1930—McNaughten, and several other spellings

9. Encyclopaedia Britannica—different spellings in different articles
10. Royal Commission on Capital Punishment, 1949, instructed by its Chairman, Sir Ernest Gowers—M'Naghten.

After all that I do not quite know what *The Times* can do if it is to desert its long standing tradition based, as you see, on a letter signed by the man himself. Perhaps it would be a nice tribute to the spirit of *The Times* if we went back to the original Gaelic.

Yours sincerely,
W. J. Haley

The Hon. Felix Frankfurter
Supreme Court of the United States
Washington 13, D.C., U.S.A.

SUPREME COURT OF THE UNITED STATES

Washington, D.C.
November 26, 1952

Dear Sir William:

Your kindness in sending me a *variorum* of Mhicneachdain afforded me another experience with the perplexities and exhilaration of scholarship. But you also raise what the lawyers like to call "a nice point." To what extent is a lunatic's spelling even of his own name to be deemed an authority?

And when you speak of "the magnificent strength of tradition" in Printing House Square, you stir in me the suspicion that the task of the Editor of *The Times* is not unlike one's job on this Court—namely, how to reconcile the conflicting demands of the needs of stability and of change. In expressing greater confidence in the ability of the Editor of *The Times* than in my own to square that circle, I speak with the bluntness that is supposed to be American.

Very sincerely yours,
Felix Frankfurter

Sir William J. Haley

«« II »»

Annual Survey of the Law

Mr. Justice Frankfurter contributed the foreword to the 1955 *Annual Survey of Massachusetts Law* (Boston, 1956), the second annual survey of the law of that Commonwealth published by the Boston College School of Law.

SURELY one of the most encouraging manifestations of aliveness in American legal studies during the last two or three decades is the proliferation of law reviews. I am not unaware of the recurring criticism that the contents of the reviews in the main fall short of excellence. To be sure, the survival value of these writings is not high. Few, extremely few, are seminal contributions of the order of the Brandeis and Warren essay, "The Right to Privacy," or Holmes' "Privilege, Malice, and Intent," or J. B. Thayer's "American Doctrine of Constitutional Law."[1] Nevertheless, as one who continues to be in the clutch of the academic habit of examining the outpouring of law reviews, even if only cursorily, I am struck with how much good there is in these reviews, considering the large number which compete for desirable contributions.

But until very recently one inadequacy could be charged against all American reviewing of the legal scene. One of

Reprinted with the kind permission of Boston College Law School.

[1] Louis D. Brandeis and Samuel D. Warren, "The Right to Privacy," *Harvard Law Review* 4:193 (1890–1891); Oliver Wendell Holmes, Jr., "Privilege, Malice, and Intent," *Harvard Law Review* 8:1 (1894–1895); J. B. Thayer, "The Origin and Scope of the American Doctrine of Constitutional Law," *Harvard Law Review* 7:129 (1893–1894).

our national complacencies is the conviction of superiority of American legal education, a pride which English scholars have from time to time encouraged, certainly at least in part, to foster schemes of educational reform in England. But in the respect relevant to the pages that follow, England had been a pacemaker, and a pacemaker behind which this country had lagged for longer than a decade.

I refer to the *Annual Survey of English Law*, beginning with 1928, which was a collaborative product of the Departments of Law and International Studies at the London School of Economics. To be sure, our law reviews have had, from the beginning, notes on the rulings of courts, comments on new legislation, and, in a few instances, reviews of contemporary legal literature. But such attention to current legal events is necessarily piecemeal and fragmentary, is concerned with trees which too often do not convey the woods. To pass under scrutiny the law for a year, in a particular jurisdiction, and to place the items in the perspective thereby afforded, promotes reflective understanding, enables one to see what is episodic, perhaps even a legal sport, and what is more permanently significant. It also brings order out of the unrelated outpouring of the legal mills and thereby fosters the harmonious development of law. Moreover, by bringing together the manifestations of explicit law-making and judicial law-shaping, emphasis is secured where it should be placed, upon the significance of all the influences that go to make up the designed pressures by which the affairs of men are finally settled.

Such were the ends that were served by the first survey of English law for the year 1928. Within the covers of an attractive book, these English law teachers gave us a critical account of case law, of important legislation, delegated as well as parliamentary, of relevant legal literature, articles and official reports as well as books, in the various domains of the great kingdom of the law. I note with deep regret that this admirable series terminated in 1940, doubtless one of the casualties of the war.

This desirable English innovation had, in its comprehensiveness, no American follower for nearly two decades. While today about a dozen American law schools, sometimes in conjunction with their state bar associations, publish what may without exaggeration be called annual surveys of their state law, one would have indeed to be blindly patriotic to find that all these are compeers of their English precursor.

Happily, the opportunity which has generously been afforded me excludes the ungracious responsibility of making invidious distinctions. Mine is the happy function of greeting the second *Annual Survey of Massachusetts Law*, given to the legal profession of Massachusetts, the larger community of the Commonwealth, and the whole world of legal learning, through the enterprise of the Boston College Law School.

Of course I have not read every word of this *Survey*. I hold that not the least of the equipment of a competent lawyer is the capacity for discriminating reading. I can truthfully say that I have adequately tested the quality of this *Survey* and can vouch for the rightness of its conception and the solidity of its execution. Its twenty-three chapters fall into three broad parts—Private Law, Public Law, Adjective Law. I must of course disclaim any specialized knowledge of any branch of Massachusetts law. But, after all, whatever its excellencies and diversities and perhaps even its rare perversities, Massachusetts law is not alien to one whose life-long concern has been law, even if one did not have an *ex officio* relation to the judicial life of the old Commonwealth. Good work scratches one, as it were, in passing and an examination even of chapters dealing with matters wholly remote from my interest engenders confidence that the statement of decisions and legislation is accurate and well balanced. We are given not merely timid recital but critical judgment. In the particular areas about which I am least ignorant, the legislation and the cases appear to be summarized with scrupulous care and they are placed in appropriate perspective.

How could this not be so, considering the fact that the various chapters were entrusted to men of established scholarship and experience in the actual administration of the various aspects of law under review. Nor is there anything parochial about the enterprise. The civilized assumption is made that different institutions of learning constitute a confraternity of scholars. While most of the authors are, and appropriately so, members of the Boston College faculty of law, the *Survey* has not moved solely within the charmed circle. It has drawn upon the available scholarship of the Commonwealth's law schools; happily it has also tapped expert understanding at the bar and among administrators.

By those to whom much is given, more is usually asked. I hope I am not unappreciative of this excellent *Survey* if I suggest that in the annuals to come there will be added a survey of the relevant legal literature dealing with the problems with which the *Survey* is concerned. And may the annuals continue so long as the reign of law prevails in Massachusetts.

III

Personal Recollections of Jonas S. Friedenwald

Jonas S. Friedenwald was one of this country's foremost ophthalmologists, both as practitioner and researcher at Johns Hopkins Hospital in Baltimore. It was at an early age, indeed, two full decades before his death, that he received the American Medical Association medal for research in ophthalmology. The following address was given at memorial services for Dr. Friedenwald, conducted at the Johns Hopkins Hospital on February 10, 1956.

In the privacy of our own feelings we are all heavy-hearted that Jonas was not allowed to run the full course. But that has not brought us together. We are not here as mourners; we are here to convey our gratitude and to reenforce and re-vivify the joy, the stimulus, the strength we can draw from his life and have drawn from it, each in his different way, throughout the years of our relations with him. I am not going to talk on any formal subject because that would not be true to our relations. It is sufficiently significant that one like myself, so far removed from his professional interests, should be privileged to speak a word on this occasion. I suppose the reason is that someone outside of his more scientific interests ought to give a sense of the amplitude, of the depth and the richness of the man who was never obscured by his profession. As Dr. Maumenee has indicated, I came to know Jonas when he turned up at Harvard (I was then on its law faculty), a youngster who already had his medical degree and had already pursued basic mathematical studies at Columbia. In a way, that was not the beginning of my relations with him. For I knew, rather intimately because of our common interest in Zionism, that benign gentleman who was his father. Very soon, however, we achieved an independent relation, for only a most obtuse mind could fail to realize that here was an extraordinary personality.

I happen to have had a good many intimate friends on the medical faculty at Harvard, younger men and older men. And it was not at all surprising for me to learn that the great Harvey Cushing detected the qualities of this young ophthalmologist and asked him to make an examination of every man in Dr. Cushing's ward at the Peter Bent Brigham. Very soon I began to realize that Jonas' interests far exceeded the boundaries, however far-stretched, of the medical sciences. He wanted to know—and this was characteristic of him—about the basic ideas of law and jurisprudence. "What can I read?" We had some talk, a good deal of talk, on and off. He wanted to know; he wanted something more than fugitive talk, and so I bethought myself and told him to read Holmes' *Common Law*. That's not an easy book—I can assure you that Holmes' *Common Law* is indeed tough going. It is not a book for freshmen but even so I gave him Holmes' *Common Law* to read, and he read it. I do not mean he passed the eye over the page. He read it thoughtfully. And I remember well saying at the time to a friend of mine: "This young doctor has asked me more embarrassing questions about some of Holmes' chapters than ever I was asked in discussion about the book by colleagues of mine on the Harvard law faculty." (And this is not a denigrating remark about the members of the Harvard Law School faculty.)

And so the years went on and he came to the fullness of his powers. Jonas and I kept up this intimacy so far as geography permitted—after all one can write, and he did come occasionally to Boston, and I did come to see him at Baltimore, and eventually I was transferred to Washington. From my early reading days I gathered something of the great controversy regarding the role of heredity as against environment: what is nature and what is nurture. In the case of Jonas he undoubtedly started with a superlative brain, superlatively unique equipment that was his, that was nobody else's. As has already been indicated, however, the two powerful forces that brought glory and developed the native, indigenous qualities of Jonas were, of course, the great tradition into which he was born and the environment which he found here at The Hopkins. I think Dr. Woods said he absorbed, must have absorbed, so much at home that in one year he acquired knowledge that it takes even good students three years to make their own. But he absorbed more than knowledge; he absorbed a comprehensive, cultured outlook on life. His father—I need not tell a Baltimore audience—was one of the most cultivated of men. His grandfather was a man of originality, pertinacity, and curiosity of mind. And his great-grandfather evidently had those qualities of enterprise and courage which in different aspects and through different modes Jonas disclosed. He revealed them in the adventures of his mind.

Then there was The Hopkins. Thanks to this occasion, I found it a liberal education to read a sizeable library on The Hopkins in order to understand the kind of environment into which Jonas came. I do not think it is a language of hyperbole that led Dr. Simon Flexner to speak, in his biography of Dr. Welch, of the heroic age of medicine. All the fortunate, fortuitous circumstances by which some people were called here—and by which some people did not come—all the enterprising genius of President Gilman, led this to be a great seed-bed of adventuresomeness, of daring, of enterprise, of enthusiasm—that great dynamo of thought—to be the place in which Jonas was nurtured. Here he had as examples men who were not just doctors but in whom doctorship was part of a full life. The great man (and enchanting creature that he must have been) Osler, was gone. But when a man like that leaves, something of him, a good deal of him, is left behind. Yet Popsy Welch was still here, and Halstead was here. I don't know whether Dr. Howard Kelly was here during Jonas' student days. But, then, he is to me more elusive. I should not suppose that culture was the dominant quality of his life. In their different ways they were all great men. They had zest, zest for inquiry. They were not confined and imprisoned, as most of us are confined and imprisoned in our respective professions. And that inquiry of Jonas': "I want to know something about the basic ideas governing law, the fruitful theories in the law," persisted in him, not only as to law, but as a good many of you know, in other domains of man's adventures. However, law continued to be a rather, what shall I say, considerable side interest of his. And I began to realize that the odd notion of the interrelation of the sciences, not only the interrelation of the sciences but of interest outside the natural sciences, was fast growing. There was a realization in educational institutions, and in the minds of men generally, that problems which theretofore had been deemed distinct imperceptibly slid one into another. Thus the great questions, not only of medicine but in law, became not merely the technical content of this or that course or this or that problem, but questions that were relevant to problems to which specialists give their lives and which become clearer by the asking of profound questions. The questions that became clearer and profounder were the common questions bearing on the creative process, how do we think what we think, what are the farther reaches of what we think.

Now law and medicine have some kinship. Law, of course, more or less reflects (usually less than more) the advances of thought in every domain. But in relation to medicine it has, of course, some immediate concerns. The criminal law, not merely its notions of insanity, but the whole domain of criminology, derives from, or is based on, assumptions which one is again and again convinced are outmoded assumptions of fact. Take the patent law. What is an invention? How do you determine what it is that has been invented? Lawyers talk about laws of nature—a phrase infected by evasions and ambiguities. What are the laws or works of nature? You can see how Jonas, having an intellectual holiday from his profession, and I, eager to get what glimpses I could of intellectual issues that were outside my daily concerns but relevant to them, would have a grand time batting balls into each other's court. And you will readily appreciate what relish and stimulation I derived from such talks. Sometimes things got put on paper. In the realm of ideas there is no hierarchy. There is not an older man and a younger man. Ideas are not ticketed according to protocol. One of the things I got out of my reading about the early Hopkins days—and I hope they still are the same—was that lines were crossed between the old and the young in adventures of the mind. Such it was between Jonas and me from the time he was a lad till the other day; sometimes it was a specific problem which I would put to him; sometimes it was a specific problem that he encountered in his reading or reflections which he would put to me.

It always seemed to me that the way to honor the memory of a man whose influence persists is to convey him in his own person. How did he express himself? What did he think when he put his slippers on; what was he like in his intellectual bathrobe? What did he put on paper when he had little thought that anybody else except the recipient would read it? With this in mind I have gone through the file of my correspondence with him over the years. And with your permission I should like to read some of his observations which give point and concreteness to what I'm trying to say about the untrammeled quality of his mind, the realization that courses are devices of educators and do not exist in nature. There are interrelations that disclose ultimate questions of concern to the lawyer, the engineer, the artist, the doctor, even the judge.

From time to time I have been troubled to understand what is really meant by "science," what consitutes "science," in any respectable use of the term. So I asked him once if he would put on paper what science is to him, and I will read his reply. I will read it to you with a great deal of confidence that it is important because a distinguished scientist to whom I passed it on was so struck with it that he asked Jonas if he might quote it in something he was writing. Here it is:

> Science is a social phenomenon. A scientific discovery does not become part of the body of science until it has been comprehended and confirmed by others. Even the most private scientific activity of the individual scientist must be based on the comprehension of what others have contributed. Consequently the language of science is as much a tool of scientific progress as any mechanical gadget which we use. If we allow that tool to be dulled, progress is slowed.

Imagine what a fruitful line of thinking and admiration that opens up to the lawyer and the judge whose tools are words and nothing but words.

> This presents a continuing problem because the advance of knowledge results in the continuous change in the meaning of words.

A whole book on constitutional law could be written with that as the legend of the title page.

When we succeed in inventing scientific words of enduring usefulness, we do so largely by naming the invariants we have discovered. In such case the advance of knowledge sharpens the denotation of our words and enriches their connotations. On the other hand, when we have not discovered the invariants we are forced to give names to evolving forms—such as sovereignty of senescence.

Think of combining in one generalization sovereignty and senescence!

Progress of knowledge on social evolution may still enrich their connotations, but, unfortunately often shifts their denotations. If we ignore these shifts, we end up by talking incomprehensively, with rich connotations, about an unspecified subject.

I canvassed a problem with him in connection with the conduct of a great educational institution, involving the relation of high scientific endeavor to the conditions under which scientific endeavor can be fruitful. Listen to this:

The talent for deliberative wisdom is most rare, I suppose, no less rare among natural scientists than among others. Perhaps one reason is that it requires some practice to develop, and our living today is so devoid of cooperative effort that we do not learn how to deliberate together. Certainly the whole training of a natural scientist is pointed in another direction. One of my old teachers used to say that the university was a place where a man with some talent for teaching was forced to do research, and a man with some talent for research was forced to do administrative work. The exceptions are the rare administrative geniuses like Popsy Welch and that wise old recluse, like J. J. Abel, one of my high Gods, who refuses to allow his administrative responsibilities to grow beyond the scope of easy and intimate management. Yet, surely, we should learn to manage our affairs more wisely for, otherwise, the [X]'s of the world manage them for us.

What are we to do about these fellows? Down here we have enough of them and I wish I could feel that the medical school does not suffer under their guidance. My own strategy has been to hew out an impregnable fortress for myself and to give advice only when I am asked. While this works fairly well, at least for the individual, in the natural sciences, I am not sure that the social sciences can be successfully promoted on such an individualistic basis.

And you will forgive this personal reference, but it is relative to my sketch of him.

So it seems to me that we need most urgently the stimulus and wisdom that you bring to this problem and it becomes very important that the painful experience with [X] should not discourage him from applying the effort elsewhere. The stakes are too important.

In one of my talks with Jonas he told me a story that sheds light on his relaxed temper of mind. His motto seemed to have been: *ohne Hast, ohne Rast,* "without haste, without rest." Serenity it is; serenity, which, I think, is hard to attain unless the good Lord has deposited something of what we call humor. I had occasion to repeat to Jonas the cynicism of a friend of mine about the medical profession. Jonas said that it reminded him of a minister, who came to see him recently, who was suffering from eczema. "He had your friend's cynicism about the medical profession and said to me, 'After all these years of medical research I do not see why your profession has not found the cause of eczema.' I offered to bet him ten to one that we would find the cause of eczema before he found why the righteous suffered."

Having read a puzzling article on a psychological matter, by a writer of considerable reputation, I asked Jonas whether the article was so obscure to me because the writer was too profound for my understanding or whether he was too muddleheaded to be clear. After analyzing some of the illogical positions taken by the writer, and, in passing, making some references to Marx and Freud and how both of them were misled by Hegel, he made this delicious comment: "No doubt economics and psychology are difficult subjects, but I do not think their difficulty is minimized by rejecting criteria for verification."

From time to time he wrote me about Supreme Court opinions and I'll read you his comments on two opinions dealing with very different subjects. One dealt with the problem of disposing of a claim of insanity intervening after a conviction for murder. The law being settled that society does not hang or electrocute an insane man, the question arose, as so often the question arises, not merely what is abstractly the right answer, but who is to determine it and by what procedure will you get the appropriate light and avoid darkness? The Court had such a case in which the question was whether a governor could decide on private advice that a man was not insane without giving the victim, or those near him a chance to be heard. Listen to this for a fellow who was ticketed an ophthalmologist:

I am intrigued by the *Solesbee* case because of the evidence it seems to me to bear on the decline of Christian doctrine. For those who do not believe in life after death there does not seem to me anything especially inhumane in executing an insane person. The argument that a person who becomes insane while awaiting execution is thereby deprived of the possibility of presenting some extenuating evidence makes sense in relation to due process [he was unafraid of these big terms, you know—he knew most of them were stuffed lines], but only at such a technical level that a violation of due process in this respect can hardly be called an offense against the basic and popularly held mores of our society. It seems to me, therefore, that the moral revulsion against execution of an insane person in the past must have had its deepest roots in the belief that the unshriven soul is damned. Evidently, this belief is not potent among the brethren nor, in their opinion, among the people of this country at large. I wish that I could feel sure that the decaying Christian morals are being replaced by something as good or better.

Then there was another case in which he thought the Court was too lenient. This is undated, but plainly it was written on one of your delightful summer days.

> It is hot and sticky down here. I have been trying this Sunday afternoon a combination of beer and electric fans, but I am beginning to think that they cancel each other out. The decision in the revocation of naturalization case is bitter medicine for me to swallow, though being a good patient I earnestly expect that it will do me good. However, to get it down I needed something of a mystic faith in the law analogous to your mystic faith in medicine. What I have trouble in understanding are the criteria by which a court decides between the obvious and simple justice in an individual instance and the principles of supposedly wider applicability.

This is about as penetrating comment on problems of jurisprudence as you can concoct.

> In this instance the choice was no doubt made easier because nobody suffers directly and personally through giving this fellow more than he deserves, but in the long run, are the general principles anything more than an aggregate of individual instances, and what bearing has that aggregate upon the exceptions which fall outside of its domain?

You will recall that he had read Holmes in his young Harvard days. Some ten years later he returned to Holmes. What he wrote me led me to suggest that he misapprehended Holmes. This was his reply:

> I see now that Holmes's contribution is much greater and more profound than I had thought, and that he has not merely followed the historical path of the evolution of the law, but has also sought and found some of those hard, bright, abstract principles which have determined the evolution. This is so far beyond anything that I had suspected that I should like very much to reread the *Common Law*. Can you suggest any elementary book which I might study first in order to familiarize myself with the meaning of the technical legal phrases which helped to obscure my understanding at the first reading?

Is it any wonder that this is the fellow who took along for his vacation reading Gibbon's *Decline and Fall* and read all the six portly volumes, and who was one of the very few people, at least in my acquaintance, who actually read all of the Toynbee and not merely ah'd and oh'd about it, or damned it at second-hand or on the basis of tidbits?

Now these are from his letters. I should like to read you two extracts from letters I wrote to him which happened to have been dictated. I read them because they illustrate his impact on at least one man whose life is spent in totally different vineyards of learning and inquiry. He sent me a rather long letter that he wrote to the *Baltimore Sun*. He was aroused by what he deemed less than adequate treatment by the *Baltimore Sun* of matters concerned with social-economic legislation. In his covering note to me he said, "I hope you do not think too ill of this. It is my first effort at polemics." In part, I wrote him:

> I take comfort in the thought that you are habituated in your primary devotion to ophthalmology and that, besides, you have an iron even if genial will. That your excellence as a painter has not diverted you from your primary allegiance to science gives me assurance that your new-found talent as a political controversialist will not divert you from your laboratory into the arena. If your correspondence with [Y] be the fruit of your first political polemic, anybody else but you would be tempted to abandon science, painting and law and all your other prior pursuits in order to become a modern Bagehot. You illustrate once more that good writing, certainly as a foundation, means having something to write about, and you certainly seem to have mastered the particular items on which you had a real case against the *Sun*.

And now let me read you the last letter that I had occasion to write him, not knowing it was to be the last. I had sent him a paper I had then recently delivered on which —believe me I'm not boasting—I had spent months of worry, reading, thought, and writing. And in that paper of some twenty-five pages he picked out for special mention the one sentence that I would on the whole have least liked to spare. And so I wrote him:

> By pouncing on the particular sentence that you hit in my Harvard Marshall Address, you remind me of your perceptiveness more than thirty years ago in matters legal. In response to your request for something that would shed light on basic legal concepts, I suggested Holmes' *Common Law,* not at all an easy book. You put some questions to me, after your reading of it, which led me to say that your inquiries were more searching than I had experienced from most of my colleagues on the Harvard Law School Faculty!

I read all this for my last sentence:

> You give proof to the truth that even the most seemingly disparate problems of the mind are not without some affinities —certainly affinities in the ways of getting understanding of them.

I said we are not here as mourners. How could we be in light of that previous quotation which three colleagues of his have given us in their memorial notice of him, his profoundly moving and intrepid words when the ominous diagnosis was made in August, expressing his "firm determination to squeeze as much joy and interest, love and meaning out of the time still available as possible." Viewed in these terms the extent of that time is a blessing for all of us. And so I say:

> Nothing is here for tears, nothing to wail
> Or knock the breast; no weakness, no contempt,
> Dispraise or blame; nothing but well and fair,
> And what may quiet in a death so noble.

IV

Franklin Delano Roosevelt

On Memorial Day, 1956, a ceremony was held at the graveside of Franklin Delano Roosevelt in Hyde Park, New York, at which Justice Frankfurter delivered the following remarks.

This is not a meeting of the American Historical Association. This is not an occasion for a documented account of the exercise of the Presidency by the only man in its history who held it for three terms and had begun the important fraction of a fourth. I shall not attempt even to sketch the significance of Franklin Roosevelt in relation to his times—the convulsions, national and worldwide, of which he was the center—the storms that he rode and how he surmounted them, the old problems that he solved, the new that he encountered and partly stimulated. I shall not indulge in the humorless impertinence of forestalling what is called the verdict of history. Indeed, Clio has the teasing elusiveness and seeming caprice of a much-wooed woman. Fluctuations of historic judgment are the common lot of great men, be they statesmen or poets—Jefferson and Lincoln, Shakespeare and Walt Whitman. It is not hazardous, however, to make one forecast. Franklin Roosevelt will meet what has been rightly defined as the final test of Presidential greatness: "To be enshrined as a folk hero in the American consciousness." He will continue to embody in an uncommonly gay and courageous manifestation the traditions and aspirations of Americans.

But if history be the ultimate judgment seat, a man's contemporaries have a special claim to be heard before it.

It has been wisely said that if the judgment of the time must be corrected by that of posterity, it is no less true that the judgment of posterity must be corrected by that of the time. Franklin Roosevelt cannot escape becoming a national saga, enshrined in myths, if you will. Myths endure only when rooted in essential truth; as such they serve to guide and sustain the high endeavors of a people. Enduring myths do not survive detached from the man who calls them forth. As it was of Lincoln, so it will be of Franklin Roosevelt, vast as are the surface differences between them. They both had the common touch—a sense of kinship with their fellows, the sense of the deep things men have in common, not common in the sense of what is vulgar and unedifying. The Roosevelt saga will never swallow up Roosevelt the man, whose friendship gave hope to millions who never knew him and whose death brought a feeling of intimate, personal loss to millions who never saw him.

Identification with his fellow men was Roosevelt's profoundest characteristic and the ultimate key to his statesmanship. He was an instinctive democrat, a democrat in feeling and not through reflection; he was a spontaneous fellow-citizen and did not become one through abstract speculation about government. More than once I was asked after March 4, 1933, "Why does F. D. R. hate the rich? Why does he have a skunner against the J. P. Morgans?" Invariably I replied, "Nothing could be farther from the truth. He isn't against the rich and the powerful. He is merely not *for* them *because* they are rich and powerful. He has the same feeling about them that he has about his neighbors in Hyde Park, pursuing their modest callings. Wealth and the power that wealth confers seemed to him negligible, indeed irrelevant, to the right feeling about them as people. Nor should it cloud our judgment regarding the consequences of their actions to society." An episode which I had the good fortune to witness right here in Hyde Park illustrates this attitude of Roosevelt's in seeing men as men. He drove up to a neighboring farmer, who for all I know may be here today, with whom he was in negotiation about a piece of land. This was in the middle thirties, when the cares of office might well have weighed down the strongest of men. The President and his neighbor entered into converse, out of earshot of the rest of us in the President's car, when I suddenly heard, what I could hardly believe I had heard, this self-respecting and self-reliant fellow American say to the President of the United States:

> Mr. Roosevelt, you and I are both very busy men. Suppose we continue this talk at some other time when we both have more time.

The President accepted this, as though it were the most obvious remark to make to the head of the most powerful nation in the world, and with the utmost good humor, he replied:

> Very well, Peter, I'll try to get hold of you some other day when you have more time.

This little episode, it seems to me, reveals more about Franklin D. Roosevelt than does many a heavily documented doctoral thesis.

Not that Roosevelt was an undiscriminating lover of his kind. His friendliness was so comprehending that his uncanny perception of the qualities of men was a less obvious trait. He was keenly aware of men's foibles and frailties, of their limitations as well as their gifts. But because he also identified himself with the frailties and foibles of his kind, he escaped the bane of self-righteousness and the corrosion of cynicism.

This permeating friendliness of Roosevelt expressed true feeling. Not less true were depths within him which were hardly accessible to anyone. From the time when he was a boy, according to his mother, he had a self-sufficiency and strength which come from the reserves of an inner life. In the light of events, his qualities of character can be deduced from the first magazine article published about Roosevelt—a delineation of him as a young state senator, in *The New York Times* for January 22, 1911, by its Albany correspondent familiarly known as "Baron" Warn. In those early days, as thirty years later in the White House, while to outward view he had a gaiety at times bordering on jauntiness, Franklin Roosevelt had a will of steel, well sheathed by a captivating smile. These reserves, deep below his outward easy-goingness, were doubtless the source and sanctuary of his resolute determination in overcoming obstacles, both in his personal life and in the conduct of affairs, that so often make men falter and not run the course. Our friend had, no doubt, the common touch. But he had also another quality—that mystical touch of grace, a charismatic quality that stirs comfortable awe, that keeps a distance between men and a leader and yet draws them to him.

What was said of Benjamin Franklin may be said of Franklin Roosevelt, that he was "a harmonious human multitude." There were fused in him the qualities necessary for leading our people out of a period of deepening economic and moral deterioration by invigorating, through precept and example, the forces of democracy. The same qualities equipped him to serve as an energy of hope for liberty-loving people everywhere in resisting seemingly invincible challenges to civilization. His sophistication gave him understanding of men. His sympathy gave him trust in them. What Winston Churchill characterized as Roosevelt's "power of gauging the tide and currents of its mobile public opinion" enabled him to govern our heterogeneous democracy. His trustfulness in them made the people return the trust.

The public issues that aroused so much rancor and conflict in the Roosevelt era will eventually, and before very long, be things of the forgotten past, as public issues which gave rise to the bitterness and passion that swirled around the heads of Jefferson and Jackson and Lincoln have become things of the forgotten past. Most political issues are ephemeral. Those leaders of our people abide who represent some universal element in the long adventure of man, represent qualities that kindle the heart and fortify the spirit. Franklin Delano Roosevelt belongs to this very small band of men who, generation after generation, accompany mankind on its fateful journey, and each of us in the gladness and gratitude of his heart is here to bear testimony to the friend who abides with us.

V

Dean James Barr Ames and the Harvard Law School

On "Law School-Graduate School Alumni Day," June 13, 1956, Mr. Justice Frankfurter returned to the Harvard Law School as a member of the fiftieth reunion class. It was on this occasion that he once again "pledged his fealty" to an institution that could never have doubted it.

THE ENTHUSIASTIC interest which the graduates of this School take in what is going on here has a quality that is, I think, rather different from ordinary alumni allegiance. This may be generally true of the relation between professional schools and their alumni. Professional alumni keep more or less current with the professional problems of professional schools. At any rate, it is, I know, deeply true of the alumni of this School, and if some of us have at times an excessively lively interest in the make-up of the faculty, in the characteristics of the curriculum, in so far as it reflects or concerns the demands of law in our society, I am confident that the Dean and the Faculty attribute such concern and its articulate expression not to the intrusiveness of busybodies but treat it as the most convincing evidence of the hold that the School has upon us, of the influence it continues to exert in our professional lives, of the place we covet for the School as the pacemaker and practitioner of the most relevant standards for legal education, as the most powerful reliance for the development of law not only for our day but for a future as far ahead as it is given the shortsightedness of man to see. As one of whom his wife says that he foolishly feels it his duty to read everything in print that falls under his eyes, I am a yearly sufferer from addresses on Commencement occasions like this. For me it would therefore be doubly reprehensible to subject you to sonorous nothingness, to labored platitudes, to rancid selfrighteousness. For different reasons, interesting indiscretions are barred. Welcome silence, the Dean's command has denied me. Since this is hardly the occasion for learned discourse, and certainly not for mere didacticism, what is there left except to vow anew fealty to the School.

It is not in a mood of nostalgia, nor as *laudator temporis acti*, that I want to speak of the Harvard Law School of half a century ago. I do so in the first place as a meager recognition of an indebtedness for one of the deepest shaping influences in my life. I find pleasure in avowing my gratitude to this place on every appropriate occasion, and surely the Fiftieth Anniversary of the Class of 1906, my class, is most fitting.

Secondly, I do so because the dominant standards and directions of the School fifty years ago have not lost their significance for the day or for the years ahead. They have weight and worth for a generation that may well find outmoded a good many—not all—of the specific rules of law that were current in the early years of this century. And since, for me, the meaning of this School is most powerfully embodied in the beloved Dean of my student days, I can best indicate what I should like to say by talking about James Barr Ames. Those of us—and our ranks are thinning—who had the very enviable experience of having been fellow-explorers with Dean Ames of the mysteries and illuminations of law will not mind having their joyous memories of Ames nudged by me. For those to whom he is merely a name, the successive classes, who entered this School year after year for forty-six years, who never saw James Barr Ames, perhaps I can increase, however little, their sense of the actuality and concreteness of a man who was the soul of this School for thirty-five years and who left the great heritage into which they came.

Maitland's maxim, "taught law is tough law," is a truth that has necessarily its very good side and its very bad side. It all depends on what law is taught or rather, more accurately, on the direction given to thinking about law. For Dean Ames it had an even deeper meaning than training lawyers to practice their profession with the highest competence. He aimed to make the Harvard Law School the center of legal influence, to make legal education the dominant force whereby law would be increasingly expressive of justice. To that end, as Dean Kirchwey of Columbia Law School observed, "He magnified the office of the law teacher and exhibited it as a career worthy of the highest talents and the most exalted aspiration for public service." As bearing on that, you will forgive a personal reference and the repetition of a story some of you have heard. In my early days on the Court, Chief Justice Hughes, on more than one occasion when at Conference he and I found ourselves in disagreement, would in a playfully mischievous way begin with "Professor Frankfurter" and quickly correct himself to "Justice Frankfurter." He indulged in this bit of whimsy just once too often when I remarked, I hope with equal good humor, "Chief Justice, please don't apologize. I know of no title that I deem more honorable than that of Professor of the Harvard Law School."

To return to my theme, Dean Ames was a creative teacher in two powerful aspects. Not merely did the work here at Cambridge, under the guiding spirit of Ames, serve as a contagious influence upon legal education throughout the country. In a more direct way, his own outlook on law and the manner of imparting it to the young was carried by pupils of his who became teachers in university law schools throughout the country. Secondly, such were his qualities that the men who went forth from this School to practice, to administer, to legislate, to judge, carried this same outlook upon law with them as eventual leaders of the bar, as participants in the conduct of affairs, as judges. Consciously or unconsciously, they imparted to their professional activities and to their civic responsibilities at least some of the qualities that Ames had evoked in them. Of course, you can't make silk purses out of sows' ears. But the potentially high qualities of the very large proportion of students who came to the Harvard Law School came, and I dare to believe still come, because of their belief in excellence, and their belief in excellence found ready vindication in Dean Ames. He awakened, stimulated, and fructified the qualities of excellence in these students. I venture to believe that of few teachers can it be said with such confidence as it can be of James Barr Ames that his own character and mind became "woven into the stuff of other men's lives."

When in 1895 Ames became Dean of this School, scholarship suffered a great loss of what he himself would have given it had he continued to remain a professor. He would rather have lightened the load of a single student or permanently awakened his interest than to have written an enduring essay or even a permanent treatise. He gave his time and thought to us, his students, with almost divine extravagance. He did not carelessly allow his day to be eaten up by the day's demands. He made the conscious choice, I believe, to make his main concern the forming of the minds and characters of lawyers and to be the stimulating force for productive scholarship among his colleagues. I could, as a mere matter of time, detain you for the rest of the afternoon with particulars that would make you realize why Dean Ames had such a unique hold upon us—why we now feel it. Two items must suffice. No lover ever guarded a cherished love letter, not Robert Browning Elizabeth Barrett's, with such treasured concern as I carried in my billfold for years, until it became scarred with age, a note from Dean Ames on which he wrote me a few words which, you will agree, are not too igniting. All it said was: "Dear Frankfurter: You gave me a good book in Trusts. Yours truly, J. B. Ames." We of the Ames era can understand the sentiments expressed in a letter which Professor Williston quoted on the occasion of Dean Ames' death. It was the letter not of an ardent young man, a student still under the fresh impact of Dean Ames, but an early student of the Dean and a man of much experience of the world:

> No other man with whom I have come in contact has made such an impression upon me, or awakened in me such a strong admiration and desire to serve. I have often thought that if the days of war were to come again with men following chosen leaders, Dean Ames is the one under whom I should want to enlist. He was the kind of man one worships and would die for. I have never felt the same about any other man I have ever known.

Ames was the great master of the case system, so-called, but he was the antithesis of the case lawyer. He did not discuss precedents much, and when he did, he analyzed them by considerations of policy. Those of us who sat in the classes of Dean Ames and had those delicious talks with him in the stacks of Austin can bear witness to the truth of John Chipman Gray's summary that it was the intellectual and moral sides of the common law that appealed to Ames. This appeal he aroused in his students. In "taking" him, as the phrase goes, and, as I did—every course that he gave, including subjects that had no intrinsic interest for me, like admiralty—one "took" not courses but the man. I know by this remark I seem to dispose of major educational problems irresponsibly. Curricular details, course offerings and requirements, teaching loads, the relation of a teacher to a subject, the cultural content of a specialty, the sources of moral influences exerted by a teacher, examination methods and such like matters imply problems about which we on the outside, merely because of devotion to the School, should not assume our competence to judge. As technical pedagogical problems, we should confidently leave them to the experience and insight of the faculty. But in so far as these implicate, as they do, more comprehensive intellectual and social concerns, they are also the responsibility of all of us. For we are all, however limited be our scope, trustees of the Law School's greatness. And the continuing greatness of the School is as important for the healthy development of the law's future as it was in the past. It is not a manifestation of the irresponsible ignorance of outsiders to reject the notion, certainly for this School, that no one is expected to know anything unless he has had a course. It is not pretentiousness to think of this School as the scientific center of the law, so long as we mean by "scientific" no more but no less than the systematic pursuit of ever-extending comprehensiveness of factors relevant to a particular problem of university inquiry. It is not, I hope, a misunderstanding of the significance of this School to wish for it to continue to make history as well as to be made by history, and, more specifically, to help shape the direction of law and not merely respond to the pressures of law in its contemporaneous manifestations.

For it will, I believe, be even more true of the future than it has been in the past that what matters most is the temper of mind in which this School sends out its graduates. The familiar simile applies to them—they are like stones thrown into a vast lake, propelling concentric circles of wide influence. These hundreds of lawyers you send forth annually affect, significantly affect, the mood and outlook of communities, of states, of the nation, through the influence they exert upon clients—clients who often are powerful industries or unions whose policies have a far and a deep reach. They are graduates who are destined for state legislatures and the halls of Congress, who cut deep into the lives of people as state and federal administrators, and who, as members of the state and federal judiciaries, not only decide controversies of great moment but, through the manner of their doing it, to no inconsiderable extent touch the thinking and feeling of the nation.

It is not, I hope, professional vainglory that makes me regard duly equipped lawyers as experts in relevance. On another occasion, when I called the roll of the best, that is, the most contributing, Secretaries of State and Secretaries of War, at a time when the Secretary of War had the triple responsibility vested in other great nations in three ministries, those concerned with the army, public works, and colonial administration, I found that it was not accident that, with possibly one exception, they were all lawyers—cultivated, intellectually disciplined lawyers.

Because he was preoccupied with seeking and promoting the ethical foundations of law, Dean Ames made rigorous demands upon hardy thinking. He eschewed looseness. His friend William James would, I am sure, have counted Ames among the tough-minded. I cannot conceive a more compassionate or generous nature than Ames'. But feeling was feeling and thinking was thinking. Difficult problems that call for the arbitrament of reason cannot be solved by question-begging or intellectual evasions. It is the tradition of this School to foster intellectual discipline. May it never relax its insistence. The bigger the slogans, the vaster the aims, the more important it is to scrutinize severely the means by which ends are pursued, or can be achieved.

The extensive breakdown of dogma in our day gives opportunities, if wisely seized, not for new dogmas but for guidance toward undoctrinaire, solidly based, even if not eternally assured, directions. Reliable directions must be founded on a passion for truth-seeking, on a courteous recognition of diversities and uncertainties. In matters sociological, including of course law, our philosophy must remain anthropocentric. Man is still at the center of our studies—what is his nature, what can it be made to be and, therefore, what was it. To treat the past as a closed book is to do so at our peril. History is not antiquarianism, nor is it the rule of the present by the past. We must look backward as well as forward. It is the function of thinkers, and I mean more particularly professors of this Law School, to discern issues before they need action. This is the place to study emergent tendencies and institutions. But the past must be assessed as a means of shedding light on the future.

To romanticize the past is to distort history. It is no better to depreciate the past. To do so is to be indifferent to the genealogy of ideas, is to fail in analysis of cultural forces. Vast convulsions have, to be sure, changed the face of the world since my classmates and I left Austin Hall. No doubt these convulsions have brought in their train problems not dreamt of by the wildest fancies of the most piercing imagination fifty years ago. As a matter of curiosity, I examined the front page of *The New York Times* of this very day fifty years ago—for June 13, 1906, also fell on a Wednesday. I won't bore you with details, but take my word for it that the items that forced their way to the front page fifty years ago were almost without exception trivia compared with the concerns stirred in us by this morning's *New York Times.* These convulsions have grown out of transforming changes, due to the great inventions and the greatly diminished hold of faith in the nineteenth century. New beliefs and skepticism about many traditional standards have made their way. These shifts in opinion have inevitably reacted upon law. But we are a little too prone to assume that the rate of change, great as it has been, has produced a complete break with the past. We are a little too prone to think that the loose, sweeping phrases that are used to describe the past or the present are accurate about either. Nothing could be farther from the truth than that those of us who were in this School fifty years ago thought of law as a closed system, as a body of unchanging rules, or that we were taught to think so by the great teachers who generated the intellectual and moral atmosphere of the School. When I hear it said that law and law-teaching should be "policy-oriented," I begin to wonder whether oblivion has overtaken Holmes and Ames and Thayer and Gray. One would suppose that O. W. Holmes, Jr. never urged that the common law was "policy-oriented" and had, from his very first writings in the early seventies, not merely announced it, but demonstrated it, with the painful labor of penetrating and, may I say, massive scholarship.

Take the field which has preoccupied most of my professional life, which is such an inviting field for much talk and less thinking. I mean, of course, constitutional law. One would suppose that it was a discovery of yesterday that the Constitution is not a code of rules in which explicit answers can be found for specific questions; but, on the contrary, that it designedly left room for inevitable changes and therefore left ample scope, though not unbridled freedom, for judges in the application of large concepts to such changing conditions. I am not unmindful of the fact that at all times in our history there have been those who have belittled the majesty of our Constitution by assuming that it enshrined forever their economic or geographic interests. A spacious view of the Constitution calls for full realization that most constitutional issues present very different elements for the process of adjudication than do cases drawing on learning of real actions. More than sixty years ago James Bradley Thayer pointed out that "the study of constitutional law is allied not merely with history, but with statecraft, and with the political problems of our great and complex national life." But he emphasized that it is so allied, namely, that in its own right and as its function it is "a body of *law*" and "therefore, it is an exact and technical subject" and not the happy hunting-ground of every penny-a-liner. Above all, it does not absolve lawyers and law professors—perhaps, I should add judges—from pursuing through much study exact and technical, in the sense of specialized, knowledge, and does not leave them free to solve difficult problems, sometimes truly heartbreaking, involving as they do the accommodation of conflicting principles with their relevant claims, by large rhetorical generalities and expansive sentiments.

Of course, there must be an adaptation of curricula to needs, but that does not tell us what are the needs. Progress does not depend on echoing the market place or congenial slogans but on pioneering. In the domain of the mind, pioneers must not be diverted by too many immediate interests of the world. They must, rather, be protected against the world's inroads; they must be protected as much as possible from the distractions of the evanescently important and from those eaters-up of time and peace which are at once the creators and the concomitants of our technological society.

This School has implanted in us a sense of what is important. It has fulfilled perhaps the ultimate function of education—to make men vibrate with wonder. What it has done in addition is perhaps of even more consequence for our day. The times in which we live have dispelled a smug belief in mankind's steady progress. But the atmosphere that this School has always created, somehow transcending professional courses, makes for readiness to do battle with the contingencies and perplexities of life, has given us an unspoken faith in endeavor, undaunted by awareness of the frustrations that so often lie in wait of hope. "A free society," it has been finely said, "is a fragile work of art only to be preserved by a combination of intelligence and moral courage." This School has had, I think I may say without boasting on an occasion like this, an honorable share in maintaining and promoting such a society. For those that follow us, let it be not an obligation but an eagerness to bear the torch passed on to us.

The Best Advice I Ever Had

This short piece was prepared in August 1956 for publication in *The Reader's Digest.* It is an example of the Justice's capacity to give life and meaning to what ordinarily would be, at best, a hackneyed topic.

ANYONE who has not in the course of his life heard some wise counsel which has stood him in good stead on particular occasions or helped to give general direction to his life must indeed be singularly insensitive or ludicrously egotistic. Most of us, I dare say, have been the fortunate beneficiaries of a good many utterances of wisdom that came to us accredited with the authority of those whom we deeply respected. I cherish several such.

It was very important for me to learn rather early in life Lincoln's attitude toward unfair criticism. "If I were to try to read," Lincoln has been quoted as saying, "much less answer all the attacks made on me, this shop might as well be closed for any other business. I do the very best I know how—the very best I can; and I mean to keep doing so until the end. If the end brings me out all right, what is said against me won't amount to anything. If the end brings me out wrong, ten angels swearing I was right would make no difference." How often men allow their energy to be dissipated and their good nature to be curdled by undue attention to baseless or unjust attacks. On more than one occasion, Lincoln's admonition has saved me from that kind of foolishness.

Again, it was altogether fortunate that I spent the formative years of my professional and public life under the late Henry L. Stimson. One of the things that I especially remember very early in my connection with him was his remark to those of us who were his assistants in the United States Attorney's Office in the Southern District of New York: "Don't waste time crying over spilt milk, except to find out why you spilt it and thereby to learn never to spill it that way again." Life is time and time is energy. This counsel of Mr. Stimson's taught me the important lesson of not wasting time and energy brooding over what cannot be undone.

Then there was a remark of Mr. Justice Brandeis that bears very deeply on the nature of man and the discipline to which one should subject himself. More than once I heard him say, "Perhaps the greatest weakness of man is his inability to say 'No.' " This weakness asserts itself in myriad ways—the weakness of not saying "No" to the temptations, sometimes far from obvious, that come one's way. There's the temptation to do as the Joneses do, the temptation of publicity, the temptation of working beyond one's strength, the temptation of unworthy ambition, the temptation to be "a good fellow," the temptation to seek or accept office because your "friends" think you ought to—temptations without end.

But perhaps the advice that has recalled itself to me most frequently and most influentially is an admonition that I had from my mother: "Hold yourself dear!" I cannot recall either the occasion or the time when I first heard her say this; it must have been while I was still in my teens. For I know that it saw me safely through those disappointments which come to so many in going through college or professional school in not "making" this or that organization, membership in which may be deemed, too often unwisely, a mark of distinction. The admonition saved me from making a deplorable decision on a crucial matter immediately after I came out of law school. A leading law firm, which with other firms, certainly in those days, would never take a Jewish law clerk, made an exception in my case. Association with that firm was highly desirable. The partner who sponsored me sincerely felt that it would promote my professional future were I to change my name for one more agreeable. He urged this on me, I am sure, out of a generous motive, saying that since I was at the beginning of my career no possible impropriety was involved. I have no doubt that my mother's advice, "hold yourself dear," made me reject the idea. "My name," I told my friend, "is part of me and I ought to respect it as part of my self-respect." Again and again those three words, "hold yourself dear," illumined situations for me, by making me realize that taking one course rather than another would subordinate important considerations in the conduct of life to unimportant ones.

One or two additional instances must suffice.

Serious doubts over the rightness of the conviction of Tom Mooney, a notorious labor agitator charged with responsibility for an explosion during a San Francisco preparedness parade in July 1916, which resulted in the death of half a dozen people, was the source of much agitation during the first World War and for years thereafter. Under instruction of President Wilson it fell to me, as counsel of President Wilson's Mediation Commission, to make inquiry into the situation. The upshot of the investigation was a report which recommended postponement of Mooney's execution so that he could be tried on indictments still outstanding in which use would not be made, as had been made in the original trial, of perjured testimony by the principal witness against Mooney. While his sentence was commuted to life by the then Governor of California, Mooney remained incarcerated despite the fact that perjured testimony was a vital ingredient of the prosecution's case against him.

A few years after the report to the President, the fairness of the investigation conducted by me was violently attacked by a nationally known lawyer who then held the distinguished office of Solicitor General of the United States. He was not content to deal with the facts of my report; he made a rather vituperative attack on my character. Considering the source, his article could hardly be left unnoticed. But the natural temptation to strike back and deal with this personal attack was suppressed by the still voice that whispered to me "Hold yourself dear." In this situation it meant, "don't get down to the other fellow's level," and so I confined myself in my reply to an austere statement of facts. It is appropriate to note that later the Supreme Court unanimously held, in an opinion by Mr. Chief Justice Hughes, that a conviction based on the conscious use of perjury by a state violates the Constitution. Eventually, the injustice of Mooney's conviction was recognized by California and he was freed.

A final incident. During the Coolidge prosperity era, when materialism was so rife in the country, I was asked to join a New York law firm at an assured income running into six figures—at least ten times my salary at the Harvard Law School. When such a temptation is dangled before one, it is easy to persuade oneself with high-minded reasons for yielding to it. Nor were the attractions of practicing law wholly of a material nature. Once more there was the inner reminder "Hold yourself dear!" It led me to conclude that to try to stimulate, year after year, influential future lawyers of the country to an understanding of their profession as public servants, merely because they were lawyers—which was the opportunity that teaching at Harvard afforded me—was a more satisfying, and therefore better, use to which to put one's life than making a lot of money at the bar. The "dignity of man" is a meaningless phrase, however well-sounding, unless one gives it concrete application in the manifold instances in which the meaning of the phrase is put to the test.

VII

The Cooper Union: Pacemaker

On October 6, 1956, the alumni of The Cooper Union gathered at a dinner to award citations to its distinguished alumni and to hear this talk by Mr. Justice Frankfurter. It was the commencement of The Cooper Union's centennial celebration. In attendance with Mr. Justice Frankfurter were two good friends, Messrs. Harrison Tweed, senior partner of a major New York law firm, and Irving Olds, a former Holmes law clerk who had become chairman of the United States Steel Corporation.

Everybody who lives in New York permanently and all visitors of this city who enjoy its amenities, are, in good truth, alumni of this institution. For I know of no other institution in this city which, through its influence over the years, has radiated the stimulus and the energy and the ambition to make New York progressively the kind of a hospitable, advanced civilized community that it is, for this great melting pot of the nation.

But, in a way, if one is to appear here in a technical role, I am two-fifths of an alumnus of The Cooper Union. Two of the great departments of this institution have been for me sources of grateful benefit through all these years. Mr. Tweed has already referred to my constant and habitual attendance at the library. I should also mention the Evening Forum Series.

When I was asked to express gratitude—which is all I undertook to do—I felt it would be ungrateful for me not to do so although the occasion for the request was a casual remark; no, not a casual remark, but a repeated remark by one of your great names in the roster of The Cooper Union benefactors. But I do not think it would be quite meet for me to say no more than to express to the present officers and trustees of this great institution, the deep indebtedness to it which I feel. In many talks I had with Mr. Gano Dunn[1] about The Cooper Union I told him that such education as I had—I can assure you one feels it is very meager—but such education as I possess is at least as much owing to The Cooper Union as to the other training institutions of which I am happily an alumnus, the College of the City of New York, as it then was called, and the Harvard Law School. Incidentally, when I consider that Mr. Olds, and Mr. Tweed, and I are all graduates of the Harvard Law School, I am beginning to wonder whether the Harvard Law School isn't a branch of The Cooper Union!

What is this institution toward which one who, through the fortuities of life, has been removed from the City of New York for many years, is still drawn in feeling? What is this institution for which we are gathered here tonight as part of an enterprise which I hope will succeed—the promotion of your forthcoming celebration of the 100th anniversary of its physical establishment? Why is The Cooper Union significant, not merely for the City of New York in the way in which I have indicated, but in the whole educational progress of the United States?

To me The Cooper Union is a pilot plant, a pacemaker, in two profoundly important respects in the role that education must play if we are to continue to approximate the ideals in which this country was founded and toward which one hopes it is moving.

[1] The late Gano Dunn was chairman of the trustees of The Cooper Union from 1935 until 1953, the year of his death.

In the first place The Cooper Union is a pilot plant, a pacemaker, in that it was established to be a nondiscriminatory institution in the sense that access to it was given to everybody, in not excluding anybody for educationally irrelevant considerations. Now, what are educationally irrelevant considerations? In the language of Mr. Cooper himself: "class, creed, race, and sex." I am not sure that those nondiscriminatory considerations are commonplaces even in 1956. But surely they were not commonplaces when the idea of this institution first burgeoned in Mr. Cooper's mind, where it began to blossom, as you know, twenty-five years, nearly thirty years, before it became a physical reality.

Of course, in those days style, the mode of expression, was different from our day—as style differs from generation to generation. They did not discriminate against the admission of women, as we now call them; they gave admission, I am quoting the language of the day, "to all respectable females." We retain the thought without the language. So that in the first place, there was this extraordinary recognition on the part of Peter Cooper that no one shall be excluded from the benefits of developing the innate qualities that nature, providence—call it what you will—gave him or her, for reasons perfectly irrelevant to the opportunities of the individual's fruition.

In this respect, Peter Cooper was not unlike, and I think he may be compared to, Thomas Jefferson. Thomas Jefferson deemed education the state's responsibility, and a university as the culminating process of a form of public education. In the case of Peter Cooper, he, of course, was the benefactor—he and his family and those who followed him—as compared to what Jefferson promoted through the Commonwealth of Virginia.

The Cooper Union was a pacemaker, a pilot plant, not only because it was available to everyone qualified to enjoy the benefits of education. It was a pacemaker also in regard to the subject matter, or the scope of education which he proposed and which The Cooper Union embodies. It was an institution for the advancement of art and science.

Just reflect on the coupling of those two great domains of human inquiry, art and science, and you will take in at once that Mr. Cooper didn't argue in his mind for a moment about an educational controversy which is as alive today as it was lively in nonpractice in his day, namely, the controversy as to education in the humanities and education in the scientific realm.

More and more we begin to realize quite obviously that if you are going to educate man you can't make that artificial distinction which is made for purposes of pedagogy and physical preoccupation, because there are only twenty-four hours in a day. You cannot make a dichotomy between education concentrating on the arts and education concentrating in the sciences in an institution for the advancement of art and science. In that respect The Cooper Union was a pilot plant. Perhaps—President Burdell can correct me, he having had a distinguished role in the Massachusetts Institute of Technology—but to me it is perfectly obvious that MIT received its stimulus, its propulsion, from The Cooper Union. It was formally established only two years after this institution, though the Civil War, of course, delayed the actual realization of the plan of the Massachusetts Institute of Technology.

Not only that, but very early, though not as early as The Cooper Union, it was true of that great institution on the banks of the Charles that they recognized that you cannot have merely technical education and produce fit and competent technical practitioners. Certainly, in my student days in Harvard Law School, it was to me an excitingly interesting fact that at Tech there were departments of history and English.

Looking at the latest, this year's Register, if that is what it is called, of the Institute of Technology in Boston, I think it is profoundly significant that they have a Department of Social Sciences with a membership of some fifty people on the teaching staff of that department; a separate Department of the Humanities with almost as large a faculty, in addition to a Department of Modern Languages.

The Cooper Union was, so far as I know, the first institution planned for the education of engineers and technicians which recognized what John Stuart Mill recognized when he said: "Men are men before they are lawyers, or physicians, or merchants," and may I interpolate, engineers. Let me continue the quotation from John Stuart Mill: "If you turn out capable and sensible men, they will themselves make themselves capable lawyers, and physicians," and may I say, engineers.

Not only all this, but Peter Cooper dedicated this institution to the continuous and social development of the life of the city through the work of the institution and the example it should serve. For he never thought of making this—as The Cooper Union never has been—a workshop or a training ground for craftsmen. This isn't the place—as it never was a place—for teaching people "knacks," "rules of thumb," mere craftsmanship.

The reason why the conflict supposed to exist between theory and practice strikes me as fundamentally unreal is that practice and theory are interrelated. Theory is the vindication, the confirmation or the discrediting of practice while practice involves the vindication or discrediting of theory. This was admirably put by Professor Whitehead, that great philosopher, when he said, in effect, that the difference between theory and so-called practice is, that the man who is preoccupied with theory has been there before. Thus, when the occasion for a practical solution to a problem arrives, there may not be time to solve it unless the man of theory has been there before.

I am told by those who know, that all the great practical advances made during the war, not excluding what may be both the greatest menace and one of the greatest hopes of man—so-called nuclear energy—that all the theoretical problems, all the theory, all the foundations on which the bomb was achieved, antedated the beginning of the war.

So, too, of some of the great medical, biological, or biochemical practical advances made in the war. I am told by those who know that practically no theoretical advance was made in the war, that the exigencies of war made people apply the theories of those who "had been there before," who had written in recondite papers known to relatively few about ideas that came into significance and effectiveness because of the demands of war.

The apparent conflicts between the humanities and science are unreal. How can you be an adequate scientist unless you see science in the social context, in the cultural context, in which and out of which the theories are evolved and in which they play their role? How can you be an adequate humanist, how can you be concerned with the functioning of man, his hopes and fears and dreams, unless you pursue inquiry into consideration of the society which is so profoundly, if not dominated, at least pervasively influenced, by the technological advance of which we are both victims and beneficiaries?

I said that I am an alumnus of this institution in two specific aspects of your five great divisions—the Library and the Evening Forum Series. I would like to say a word about each. You remember Keats' sonnet, "On First Looking into Chapman's Homer," celebrating an experience like seeing and discovering the ocean for the first time? Well, that is the way I felt. I didn't know either Keats or Homer or Chapman when I discovered the reading room of The Cooper Union. But the feeling and emotion it stirred in me must have been of a similar kind.

It wasn't merely that it was a warm room and the streets were cold, though there were those who found that not an unattractive aspect. But the notion that I could read all the papers of the United States, that there they were and I had the opportunity to read them, was exciting. It set me afire. I don't know whether I was there four days—four afternoons a week, or five. I think it was not less than four days a week, that my feet found their way up to the reading room.

There I was—and I spent hours, I sometimes think wastefully—in reading all those papers. I don't mean I read them all but there was a time—it has long since passed—that if you gave me a scrap of a newspaper I could tell whether it was the *Emporia Gazette* or the *Louisville Courier-Journal*. I think it was a wonderful thing to make that available to people like me, situated as I was, representing as I did that—what shall I say—that multinational life that the City of New York was then, and perhaps still is.

Mr. Tweed said we lived on Seventh Street—we did, Ninety-nine East Seventh Street. Since my people were from Vienna we naturally moved into a German neighborhood. But closely impinging was an Italian neighborhood and the various other nationalities; the Chinese were not far away. Without any formal propaganda about Americanism, without any fustian talk about loyalty, you just breathed in the sense that this was the America one had heard about, the land of freedom, the land of opportunity.

To me—I didn't spell it out, of course, in those days—not being like that kid who at twelve had entered Harvard—I couldn't help but unconsciously imbibe something which later I realized does signify America as we know it, in comparison with some of the totalitarian regimes where the first thing they did was to abolish a free press. That there should be one place in this city where people could come to—and free of charge—read the papers of all the rest of the cities, was a very great thing, a very great nurturing of what America means in the mind of not only myself but—I haven't the slightest doubt—of hundreds and hundreds who went to the reading room during these many years, after I ceased to go there, because I left schooling in the City of New York and went to Cambridge, and then eventually to Washington.

There was a minor thing about that reading room that is important. As I read the record of The Cooper Union, there was a great deal of debate whether the Library should be available—there were, of course, books—whether the library should be available to all the Toms, Dicks, and Harrys like myself or whether it should take some precaution against inevitable mutilations because occasionally some people were so fond of the brilliant things, the exciting things they read, that in a vandalic way they cut them out. To the great wisdom and glory of those people who then ran The Cooper Union—I hope it is still true—there were no restrictions upon the reading room, on the theory that the evil a few people do is worth the price of not restricting the good that may come to the many.

Many years ago I went through one of the loveliest of library buildings in this country—the Library at Dartmouth College. A classmate of mine was showing me around. On the top floor of the library building—those of you who have been there know it—I saw students smoking. I said to my friend, Professor Ames, "Hello, I congratulate you on the good sense of letting students smoke. How did you manage it?" "Well, we had quite a row, because there were always fellows on the faculty who said, if you let students smoke they might set fire to something or other; and those of us who thought that it is better that an occasional book should be set on fire by an occasional student than discourage them from using the library by prohibiting smoking." There, again, I think The Cooper Union was a pacemaker. I don't think there was another library in the United States in 1859 or 1860 that was so free in the use of books—let alone the newspapers—as was the Cooper Union Library.

Let me talk about the second aspect—so important in my life and for which I am so deeply grateful that I am subjecting you to these remarks—that is the Forum, the evening meetings in that Great Hall. In my day that Great Hall had red leather chairs. That was the day before red was a smearing color. I hope the chairs have remained red, Mr. President.

The Forum was a great center for realizing Cooper's conviction that talk is what makes democracy go, interchange of minds, free talk. But talk isn't enough. Talk must be based on reflection. Talk must be based on study. So he provided both the studies and opportunity for talk.

In my day the meetings that I particularly attended were Friday night sessions, then known as the Peoples' Institute of which Charles Sprague Smith, whose name should always be associated with the work of The Cooper Union, was Director. On Friday night, all the public issues of the day were canvassed.

I remember many a cold day, many a snowy night, when the queue was long, waiting for those doors to be opened, because people were so eager to listen to the speaker on some issue of the day, a condition of which was that the questioning period should be just as long as the orating period.

That part of the work of The Cooper Union, The Peoples' Institute, was established—if my memory is not betraying me—in 1897. It was largely made possible by Mr. Abram S. Hewitt who regarded it with much skepticism. He didn't think that this strange creature, Charles Sprague Smith, a professor at Columbia and a specialist in the Icelandic language, who proposed it, would succeed. But Mr. Hewitt felt very strongly that the idea of Peter Cooper required that The Cooper Union should be a radiating center in the continuing education of the people of the City of New York in its social and economic problems, and that it could be best advanced by having a speaker and a questioning period after the speaker.

Of course, I don't have to remind you that The Cooper Union has a historic place in the political history of the United States, because it was in The Cooper Union on February 27, 1860, that Abraham Lincoln made his great speech. I re-read it only two days ago by way of refreshing my recollection. It was a speech that made his name, which made him known in the East for the first time and had not a little to do with his nomination in Chicago a few months later.

I speak out of a deeply grateful heart for what The Cooper Union has been to me personally. I am sure I represent thousands and thousands of people who, while they formally cannot be claimed as members of your Alumni Association by virtue of a degree from your institution, feel that they are part of your history.

I have, in a manner of speaking, had actual relations with two of your founding fathers, two of the six men who were the original trustees of the institution. When I say personal relations, I am using the word in a loose sense.

I did not have personal relations with Mr. Abram S. Hewitt, but through all my boyhood he was the first citizen of New York. He died in 1903, just as I went to the Harvard Law School. From the time I was brought here as a boy until then, Abram S. Hewitt was the first citizen of this great city. Somehow or other a great man makes everybody else feel a little bit great. One has that association that I had through consciousness of the fact that when Mr. Hewitt spoke one felt that the voice of wisdom had been uttered.

One other original trustee I did know, face to face. I was actually on the other side of a counsel table from Mr. John E. Parsons who also was one of the original trustees and who, I believe, drafted the charter for the institution. To be sure, Mr. Parsons was a very eminent lawyer when I was an obscure young lawyer almost fresh out of law school. The fact is, however, that one of the charms of the legal profession is that we call one another brothers, and that, too, sometimes in a very loose sense. The fact is I remember Mr. John E. Parsons as a man of force, of culture, of civic pride, and of civic achievement.

Which leads me to say that your present trustees—I do not want to bring blushes to their hardened modest cheeks—but I suspect it is true of them—for I happen to know two of them—it is true of them as one of the biographers of Mr. Cooper says was true of the original trustees, that they devoted their time and their thought to the institution, not out of a "surfeit of leisure" but out of a sense of civic responsibility. Institutions are men. Educational institutions are essentially the faculty. But the trustees, at worst, ought not to interfere and at best should collaborate with the work of the faculty, as is true of The Cooper Union.

One word more and I am done. Mr. Cooper, in language reflecting the age in which he was born and brought up—for he was after all a child of the Age of Enlightment—said he hoped this institution would be "an inspiration of truth in all its native power and glory."

We are not as sure as Mr. Cooper was that truth is so easily had, so easily as those men thought it was. We now know a great deal more about the nature of man, the deep dark unconscious recesses out of which actions come or by which actions are thwarted. We also know the questionable, the dubious, the precarious implications of modern technological development in so far as they have given us mass media and the things of the human mind. Mass media may produce mass minds.

I do not think that history records that great progress is attributable to the operation of mass minds. The history of civilization, I suspect, is to no large extent the history of minority thoughts, the history of dissidents, the history of nonconformists. If everybody reads the same thing and hears the same thing and is infected in the same way, those impulses to originality and individuality upon which the progress of mankind depends are likely to be stifled and retarded, if not prevented.

So I say, if I may somewhat modify Peter Cooper's words, instead of hoping for your institution to be the inspiration of truth in its "native" power and glory, *truth has to be pursued, truth has to be coaxed, truth has to be won. It isn't given.*

So I wish for your institution, Mr. Chairman and Mr. President, the continued zealous pursuit of truth, so that not only through what you do here, but through the continuing example that you set for the country by the pursuit of truth, you will promote reason and justice throughout the land.

«« VIII »»

Louis Dembitz Brandeis

In commemoration of the centennial of the birth of Mr. Justice Brandeis, Mr. Justice Frankfurter wrote the following article, which appeared in *The New York Times Magazine* on November 11, 1956, under the title: "The Moral Grandeur of Justice Brandeis."

Of the eighty men other than Mr. Justice Brandeis who have sat on the Supreme Court, oblivion has overtaken most of them. In saying this I speak with reverence for the Court's role in our society and with the respect of a lifetime's study of its history. I do not minimize the share of the least remembered in the collectivity which, as a Court, has been engaged in the intricate and enduring process of making of our Constitution living law.

But at the moment I am concerned with greatness, and greatness is a rarity, whether in art or in science, whether on the bench or in the scholar's chair. The fact is that of these men surely not more than a half-dozen either created for themselves a place in the national consciousness or made an impress on the jurisprudence of the country or merely extended on the Court the contribution to social thought and action they had made before coming there. All three claims can confidently be made on behalf of Mr. Justice Brandeis, the centenary of whose birth falls this Tuesday.

Speaking out of a friendship of more than a half century and with an understanding not exceeded in our legal history, Mr. Justice Holmes passed this judgment on Mr. Justice Brandeis, on the occasion of the latter's seventy-fifth birthday: "Whenever he left my house I was likely to say to my wife, 'There goes a really good man.' I think that the world now would agree with me in adding what the years have proved, 'and a great judge.'" Certainly no one entitled to an opinion would disagree. The significance of this estimate derives only in part from Mr. Justice Holmes' habit of measured praise. What underlines it is the validity of his view that there have been fewer instances of truly great judges than of great men in almost any other department of civilized life.

Yet, when President Wilson on the Friday of January 28, 1916, sent to the Senate the nomination of Louis D. Brandeis as associate justice of the Supreme Court of the United States, it brought forth a storm of opposition whose ferocity was unequaled in judicial nominations, barring possibly Jackson's nomination of Taney. Seven former presidents of the American Bar Association denounced Brandeis as "not a fit person to be a member of the Supreme Court." These distinguished lawyers did not oppose the nomination because Brandeis had never been a judge before. They knew the history of the Supreme Court too well not to know that judicial experience as such is not a qualification nor a desideratum for the Court's work; the problems which predominantly come before the supreme bench are of a different order from the staple business of other courts. The opponents objected, rather, to Mr. Brandeis' career at the bar—the standards by which he was guided, the causes which he had championed, the outlook which he manifested on the law's relation to life. It may fairly be said that the qualities and conduct which led President Wilson to make Mr. Brandeis a personal selection for the Court animated the zeal of those who opposed him.

One refers to this episode—an important episode—in our history, not to rekindle the feeble embers of a conflict that had best be forgot. But it is important that the episode itself be not forgotten, because it bears on an adequate analysis of qualifications for the court and of the influences that shape understanding of them.

It is no paradox that he who so quickly attained recognition as one of the giants of the Court should have aroused the hostility of the old leaders of the profession. For months a Senate committee heard testimony about some aspects of Mr. Brandeis' private practice. But beneath the dreary details lay those deep socioeconomic issues which are personified by Theodore Roosevelt, the elder La Follette, and Woodrow Wilson. The nomination of Louis D. Brandeis to the Supreme Court was one of the manifestations of those great developments in our society which came to the fore on Theodore Roosevelt's succession to McKinley. New economic and social forces are inevitably reflected in litigation before the Supreme Court. The nomination of a man with so powerful an intellect as Brandeis', and one who had given such striking proof of not being partial to the current dogmas, was bound to awaken the distrust of those who felt the familiar to be the necessary.

In his early years at the bar, Mr. Brandeis differed from other successful lawyers only by the rapidity with which he attained professional success. But as time went on, he became rather a lawyer apart, in the sense that he saw the deeper social and economic problems of which his client's difficulty was merely a phase, and having seen them, probed the case to its depth. Increasingly, he identified himself with the public aspects of what were apparently private controversies. He inevitably disturbed inertia, blindly entrenched power, and complacency.

His was a disciplined, highly cultivated mind, passionately devoted to the rule of law as unfolded in Anglo-American constitutional history, bent on conserving the fruits of civilization and desirous of enhancing them, joined to a compassionate nature that was sensitive to injustices and rejected the notion that whatever is, is right; all this was gradually transmuted by the processes of modern propaganda into a public image of a demagogic radical. To those not blind to the facts, it did not require the demonstration of his judicial career to render this picture grotesque. Mr. Brandeis was sixty years old when he came to the Court, and by that time the lines of his intellectual and moral outlook were deeply laid.

Mr. Justice Brandeis came to the Court not only without any prior judicial experience—that is true of some of the most outstanding men who have sat on the Court—but he is one of the very few who came to the Court without having had the experience of any public office, being in this regard, as in other aspects, like another great figure in the court's history, Mr. Justice Joseph P. Bradley. Never was there, however, an easier transition from forum to bench than when Mr. Brandeis became Mr. Justice Brandeis. Indeed, his work on the Court may fairly be described as a continuation of preoccupation with those exigent social and economic problems which had engaged his mind long before his judicial career.

To be sure, the nature of his concern with these problems changed considerably. He now had to move within the narrow confines of the judicial function, either in reviewing the power of the executive and legislative branches of the Government, national and state, or in construing legislation and fashioning law within the limits open to the judiciary. But in exercising the restricted powers of the judiciary, the quality of understanding he brought to the problems involved in litigation before the Supreme Court between the two world wars largely determined the wisdom of its adjudications.

As a lawyer who saw a legal question in the context of its meaning in the affairs of life, and as a citizen who had given himself to grappling with matters of great public concern, Mr. Justice Brandeis had for years been immersed in the problems which modern industry and finance had created for our society. The experience which he had acquired, bearing on the kind of conflicts which came before the court during his incumbency, was not excelled if indeed equaled by any lawyer of his time. Having a firm grip on their details and having extracted their significance, his mind moved freely amid the intricacies of large affairs —railroading, finance, insurance, public utilities, the conservation of natural resources, industrial relations.

At a time when our constitutional law was becoming dangerously unresponsive to important social changes, when decisions were rested on hollow formulas, themselves the product of limited experience, he insisted, as the great men of law have always insisted, that law must be sensitive to life. "*Ex facto jus critur,*" he wrote in a very early opinion. "That ancient rule must prevail in order that we may have a system of living law."

How he employed the powers of his mind and the experience which it had garnered had best be put in the authoritative statement of Chief Justice Hughes made while the two were still active members of the Court:

> It is expected that those selected for the highest judicial offices in state and nation should have keen minds and analytical skill tested by long experience, and there will be no dissent from the opinion that Mr. Justice Brandeis possesses that acuteness in a very high degree. No keener blade has ever been used, but it is the knife and skill of the surgeon exploring

the operations of the social organism with the purpose of cure. The combination of this analytical power, with a talent for comprehensiveness and a method of expression, which comes as near to being original as is possible under a rare and, I might say, a unique distinction to his judicial work.

Since the litigation that comes before the Supreme Court is so largely entangled in public issues, the general outlook and juristic philosophy of the justices inevitably will influence their views and in doubtful cases will determine them. This is saying something very different from the too prevalent notion that divisions on the Court run along party lines. Such divisions reflect not former political attachments but convictions of the judges about government, their conception of our Constitution and, above all, their philosophy of the judicial function in general and in the particular context of our federal system.

Such enumeration of the large considerations that come into play in a particular exercise of the judicial process by the Supreme Court is a compendious statement of many complex and subtle factors. Merely to analyze them needs the scope of a book. To attempt to state pithily what needs detailed elucidation is a hazardous enterprise, especially regarding the work of a judge like Mr. Justice Brandeis. For, while metaphysical speculation was not congenial to him and he distrusted ideologies of all sorts, juristic or otherwise, his judicial life reveals a coherent, carefully wrought juristic philosophy, relevant to the place of the Supreme Court in the American system as the means of promoting a society that should adequately fulfill the potentialities of its citizens.

His own experience and deep study confirmed the impress left on him by the influential teaching of Professor James Bradley Thayer that the Constitution has within itself ample resources for meeting the changing needs of successive generations. Within its defined limits the Constitution affords the country, whether at war or at peace, powers adequate for the life of a great nation. Our federal system was for him not an outmoded historical mechanism. In its distribution of governmental powers he found comfort for his fear of bigness as a menace to individual fulfillment.

Mr. Justice Brandeis was captive to no dogma. Final truth was the unattainable bottom of an unfathomable well. But just because the efforts of reason are so tenuous the constant process of critical scrutiny of the tentative claims of reason seemed to him essential to the very progress of reason. Knowledge will advance and truth enlarge its domain only if error may freely be exposed. Error will go unchallenged if dogma, no matter how widely accepted or dearly held, may not be questioned, however crudely. If men cannot speak and write freely they will soon cease to think freely.

Passionately as he believed in the unfettered exercise of the mind, Mr. Justice Brandeis was no doctrinaire in regard to this essential freedom of a free society. He powerfully vindicated its claims and gave it generous scope, but refused to make even freedom of speech an absolute. It is not without significance that in the very case in which Mr. Justice Brandeis gave most eloquent expression to his conception of the historic identification of this country with the fullest opportunities for the exercise of the free human spirit, he sustained a conviction for an abusive exercise of that right.

Great men live on in the lives of other men. Rarely is this true of a great judge. But it is conspicuously true of Mr. Justice Brandeis. While still at the bar, he deeply influenced others, the obscure and the highly placed, by his example and the stimulus of fructifying encouragement. The range of his influence was enlarged after he came on the Court.

Deserving of specific mention is the intellectual partnership, as it were, that he formed with his succession of gifted law clerks. In them he lighted the torch, not of any particular cause or ideological commitment, but of the pursuit of civilized life. In their various ways, these men have achieved the personal significance which for Mr. Justice Brandeis was the only true test of success. What he meant to these, as well as to others whose lives he touched, is indicated by the words of one of them: "His was the quality that by a word could lift the heart, and by a nod enkindle the spirit."

We cannot turn to great men for answers to specific problems that were not theirs. They do not represent socio-economic prescriptions. They do serve as guides for the large-mindedness and the generosity of spirit with which problems must be met. For the essential conditions of wisdom, whatever the demands upon it, are large-mindedness and generosity of spirit. Everything that was mean and petty and intolerant, everything that emphasized the evanescent as against the enduring, was ruled out by Mr. Justice Brandeis' life. It was ruled out because it was irrelevant to the wise conduct of life.

The striking likeness between Mr. Justice Brandeis and the beardless Lincoln was a matter of familiar comment. The environment, the upbringing, the experience, the whole cultural past, could hardly be more different for two men than they were for these two Kentuckians. But the magic and mystery of personality is such that the spiritual kinship between these two men was even more striking than the similarity of their faces.

There was about Brandeis, as about Lincoln, a moral grandeur without the slightest taint of self-righteousness. Moral distinction is felt, like great poetry, and like it, finally eludes analysis. But one can account, at least in part, for this spiritual authority in Brandeis and in Lincoln as an achievement of self-discipline, the product of will in the service of wisdom that was steadily enhanced by disregard of self beyond the capacity of ordinary mortals.

IX

Woodrow Wilson

Felix Frankfurter knew President Wilson personally, if not intimately, by reason of Frankfurter's service in Wilson's administration in a variety of posts that included attendance at the Peace Conference at Versailles. The following essay was published in *The Times* (London) on December 28, 1956, on the occasion of the one-hundredth anniversary of Wilson's birth.

Some judgments about Woodrow Wilson may be expressed with certitude. Not that the passions he aroused in his own day are spent. Idolators and detractors are still about. But whatever may be the fluctuations of historical verdict, Wilson will surely join the company (the Father of his Country apart) of his three greatest predecessors—Jefferson, Jackson, and Lincoln. This distinction can hardly be based on what has appealingly been laid down as the final test of Presidential greatness: "to be enshrined as a folk hero in the American consciousness." There appears no foreknowledge that Wilson will attain such a homely and endearing significance in the feelings of the American people. His stature in the history of his country derives from the fact that he permanently influenced the direction of its affairs both within itself and in its global relations. (It ought to be noted that President Theodore Roosevelt, even more than President McKinley, first took the United States into the world.)

Wilson's place in world history is tied to the fate of the ideal for the promotion of which he gave his life — organized peace. If it be the destiny of mankind increasingly to adjust by rational methods the inevitable clash and confusion of interests among the different peoples of the world, however agonizing the travail and checkered the efforts, Woodrow Wilson's name will surely be recognized as one of the most eloquent and resolute promoters of such a consummation. If, on the other hand, an era more ghastly than the Dark Ages is to be the lot of man, Wilson's fame will be obscured by it and his name will survive only as a nourishing hope to those who will start anew the toilsome journey toward reason.

Woodrow Wilson is the only man who came to the Presidency not from the world of affairs but from Academe. His governorship of New Jersey was a brief episode in his life as scholar and university president. But while he was a novice in politics, it is not the least striking evidence of Wilson's extraordinary self-direction that he is one of the few men to attain the Presidency who planned it that way. Though he was a dedicated scholar and a prolific author, after a brief, unhappy attempt at the law, his reputation as a scholar, barring only a single book—his first, *Congressional Government*—would but for the Presidency have been ephemeral. His political philosophizings, conveyed through agreeable essays, were dilutions more than distillates of Burke and Bagehot, his acknowledged masters. To suggest that in weighty learning he was exceeded by the two Adamses and that Jefferson's intellectual legacy to political thought far outweighs Wilson's is not to dispraise him. Nor would his headship of Princeton University have given him, with all due regard to the introduction of the preceptorial system and the general ferment that he imparted to major educational problems, the enduring reputation of President Gilman of Johns Hopkins or President Eliot of Harvard.

These qualified achievements in the life of his choice make all the more striking the speed with which he asserted resolute and effective executive leadership in the White House. He did this dramatically at the very outset of his administration by appearing before Congress on April 8, 1913, in person, thereby reviving a practice which Jefferson had allowed to lapse because he lacked the gifts of a public speaker. Throughout his administrations, until he was stricken, Wilson was the focus of governmental power. He is the classic example of strong executive leadership in discharging the responsibilities of the vast power inherent in the mere existence of a nation like the United States as well as of the need for Lincolnian forbearance and compassionate wisdom with which it must be exercised to avoid obstructive opposition by Congress.

This is not the occasion to speak in detail of Wilson's domestic policies and achievements. The ominous concentration of economic power following the Civil War and the disregard of its social implications started reform movements to which Theodore Roosevelt gave national expression. Further impulse to these efforts was furnished by the frustrations and resistance aroused by Taft's lethargic administration. President Wilson put himself at the head of these reforms.

In his concern with these domestic issues, Wilson was on more or less familiar ground. But with sombre premonition he remarked shortly before going to Washington, "It would be the irony of fate if my administration had to deal chiefly with foreign affairs." His fear was promptly fulfilled. Mexico, China, Japan, the Philippine Islands, and Nicaragua presented exigent difficulties which, wrote Ray Stannard Baker, his admiring biographer, "he approached with little actual knowledge of conditions." Some even more deeply rooted and obdurately tangled European conflicts of interests and appetites could not be kept away by the separating Atlantic, and he had also shown little concern for these historic conflicts and their contemporaneous persistence.

From the outset, he was determined not to become embroiled in the ensuing first World War. "The people count on me," he said, "to keep them out of war." But it hopelessly misses the nature of the man to find explanation for this attitude in pusillanimity or in a pacifistic shrinking from the shedding of blood. Even as did Lincoln in the midst of the Civil War look beyond to the inevitable day of settlement, so Wilson in his way wanted to preserve for the world the power of "disinterested influence over the settlement" which the United States as a noncombatant would, in his opinion, be capable of exerting.

"By slow merciless degrees, against his dearest hopes, against his gravest doubts . . . he was forced to give the signal he dreaded and abhorred." This summary by Sir Winston Churchill of the process by which President Wilson asked Congress for a declaration of war is, if one may say so, an accurate analysis. "But nothing," Sir Winston continues, "can reconcile what he said after March, 1917, with the guidance he had given before. What he did in April, 1917, could have been done in May, 1915." Could it? The remoteness in feeling of the American people, even apart from its multiracial population, about the European imbroglio, made it necessary for Wilson to have a substantially united country behind him whenever the force of circumstances, greater than his own determination, should leave him no choice. Once Wilson concluded that Imperial Germany was an international criminal all his doubts and scruples against entering the contest as a belligerent were gone. It can hardly be gainsaid that when the time arrived he was as cleansed, and convinced the nation that he was as cleansed, of narrowly interested or vainglorious motives as any statesman that took his nation to war.

Wilson, like Lincoln, could not separate the effective conduct of a war from its aims. The generous and noble terms in which he expressed those aims sustained the fighting spirit of tired peoples and filled the whole world with hope. He came to be regarded with an adulation, indeed veneration, that should have been frightening to a mere mortal. It was not calculated to temper his feelings of self-sufficiency. Nor did it tend to enlarge his appreciation of old antagonisms and newly whettled appetites of the war-weary European combatants. He was confident that he could project, as C. P. Scott put it, his ideological images onto the world at large and give them international validity. As merely an "associated power," and not an "ally," he was heedless of the self-seeking commitments made among the "allies." He was confident that with the support he had aroused in peoples everywhere, the vision of his will would subordinate all lesser interests, and so he kept himself, as he thought, free from all arrangements for the eventual settlement while he wielded indispensable military power.

When the time came for translating his hopes into a treaty, he surely started with a fatal mistake by going to Paris in person. In Washington he could thunder from Sinai. In Paris he was only one among a group of negotiators, negotiators better equipped and much more experienced in the art. Wilson's share in the Paris peace talks embroils one in all the perplexities of his personality. The sophisticated artist in Maynard Keynes may have overdrawn his famous portrait of Wilson at the Paris Peace Conference; a caricature it is not. Woodrow Wilson was a Presbyterian Covenantor. He had vision and determination, but he repressed any sense he may have had of the "many-colored passions of life." Lincoln, too, might have refused to visit the battlefield at Verdun, but he would not have done so with self-righteous brusqueness.

The man who deemed Walter Bagehot a "seer" paid little heed to Bagehot's central recipe for a liberal society—namely, that it be a "polity of discussion," and this though phrases like "the common counsel of the nation" and "laying mind against mind" were frequently on his tongue. Wilson said of himself that "seeing people debilitates me." Devoted as he undoubtedly was to mankind, he kept aloof from personal contacts. His Secretary of State had to beg for an interview and his Ambassador to London waited for five weeks in Washington before he could see his chief. His closest confidant and the most obeisant servant of his master, Colonel House, never could discover why he was cast into limbo. Wilson was guided by an inner light, and an inner light which he too often failed to vouchsafe to those whose devotion he most cherished. Thus, Secretary of War Newton D. Baker, his favorite Cabinet member, did not know of the decision in the ill-starred Siberian enterprise until he was asked to sign the formal order for moving the troops, although Baker was known to view the military justification for such action as baseless and its political consequences dangerous.

To these, at least as yet, inscrutable aspects of Wilson's nature, we must look for explanation of the defeat of his own greatest cause, the organization of peace through agencies and processes of reason, of which the Covenant of the League of Nations was to be the great instrument. Whatever the ups and downs of historical verdicts, it will be surprising if there should ever be substantial disagreement from the conclusion of President Charles Seymour of Yale that "a few conciliatory gestures by the President would have sufficed to win the two-thirds vote necessary to ratification." One must hazard a guess that Wilson had an impairment of his vitality, which in a subtle way affected his judgment, long before his breakdown in September 1919. On no other basis can one explain some of his errors —misjudgments of a kind alien to his habit and outlook— though others were functions of his nature.

Temporarily at least he lost his cause. But Sir Winston Churchill, after severe criticism of President Wilson's part at Paris, has, with characteristic generosity, written his epitaph: "However as Captain he went down with his ship."

«X»

On Entering the Law

Mr. Justice Frankfurter was repeatedly asked for advice on the question who should entertain the choice of a career at law. In this case, the advice was published in February 1957 as one of a series of articles entitled "Guide to Career Opportunities," in *The Harvard Crimson.*

THE BEST reason for going into the law is the same that led Fritz Kreisler to be a fiddler and Gutzun Borglum to be a sculptor—some inner compulsion that selects one's career. Fortunate indeed are those for whom a coercive aptitude or a controlling interest leaves no problem for choice of a calling. So far as the law is concerned, I suspect this inevitability saves less than the majority who are finally won to the law from the painful necessity of choice. Indeed, the probability is that a much larger percentage of men turn to the law in default of not clearly being enticed by some other activity. Men have attained preeminent distinction in the law who took it up with dubiety and even with grave misgivings. Thus it was years before Mr. Justice Holmes came to rest in the conviction that "a man may live greatly in the law as well as elsewhere." I assume that in asking us to speak about our respective professions to those who have to make conscious choices, we are addressing men who are concerned with a life and not with a living. Only very rarely, I suppose, does a man decide between law and one of the arts, for, to quote Mr. Justice Holmes once more, "the law is not the place for the artist or the poet." Even so, I have known at least two instances of men buffeted between their love for music and the seductions of the law. And Edgar Lee Masters and Archibald MacLeish attained their fame as poets after they demonstrated high competence at law. But these are rare exceptions. Those who are not fortunate enough to go into the law as a matter of course, in response to an inner call, are likely to be men who have no fierce drive in any other direction, whose abilities are of a diffused or as yet undefined nature. In resolving their doubts and uncertainties, they will appropriately ask what kind of reasonable hopes for fulfillment of one's endeavors and dreams does the profession of the law hold.

Since everything is connected with everything else in the universe, if one only pursues the interconnections, nothing is sillier than to make competing claims of intellectual interest for one profession as against another. But one is surely not guilty of guild parochialism in asserting that the law affords the amplest opportunties for the greediest intellectual appetite. The law has fairly been called a great anthropological document. It reflects and to no small degree embodies perhaps the significant achievements of civilization, putting to one side, of course, the finest flowers of civilization—the great works of poets and artists. The fact that these profounder aspects of law lie beneath the surface of the daily concerns of the men of law makes the intellectual adventure to which the law beckons all the more exciting.

These intellectual interests do not center about abstractions. The law's concern is society, men and women. And so, whether in the daily life of practitioners or in the context of the history of institutions and ideas without which law is a grab-bag of unrelated rules and episodes, law throbs with human interest: it touches the fate of man in all his vicissitudes of joy and sorrow, of mean pursuit and high adventure. The pageantry of Anglo-American legal history for nine hundred years is visible to the understanding eye of the law of today. Whether in the heavy-carpeted suite of a big New York firm or in a small-town office, the lawyer is afforded the satisfactions that come to those who help guide others through the complexities and hardships of life.

But when one speaks of these human satisfactions of a lawyer one must quickly add the variety of men of law that there are, the diverse ways in which one may vent one's powers in the law. Predominantly, of course, there are the practising lawyers—the men of whom I have just spoken, the men who counsel others in the wise conduct of their affairs, the men who defend and protect life, liberty, and property and thereby further the pursuit of happiness. Then there is the increasing number of law teachers, experiencing the happiness that their function brings. We do not in this country, as is true in Continental Europe, train men explicitly to become judges. But lawyers do become judges by the thousands in this vast land, with the deep satisfactions that the judicial office implies. Again, increasing outlets for lawyers are the administrative agencies, in the states and the nation, at a time when legislation and therefore administration have some say in the lives of men from the cradle to the grave.

The extensive utilization of lawyers in governmental affairs is due not merely to the fact that we are predominantly a legal society, that our society moves within legal frameworks—the United States and the state constitutions. The reason, I believe, is deeper. Fundamentally, it is the same reason that men of law often become the guiding heads of great enterprises and predominate in politics. The reason was thus put the other day in accounting for the fact that Great Britain selects for the chairmanship of governmental inquiries into perplexing problems the best exemplars of the legal profession:

> This country, more perhaps than any other, is in the habit of using its eminent lawyers and judges in capacities seemingly far outside their profession, as chairman of Royal Commissions or similar bodies, for purposes not only of investigating facts, but of the weighing up of the state of argument in major political or economic controversies, and the preparation of long-term policy decisions . . .
>
> The reasons for such extra-mural appointments of judges are not only that judges can naturally be supposed to be "judicial" in the sense of being impartial when faced with contending interests or arguments. It is rather that the legal profession at its highest level does, as probably no other, develop the absorptive and analytical capacities of the human mind.[1]

I should deeply regret if the claims I have made for life in the law sound vainglorious or exclusionary. A far better insight than any words of mine can convey into the potentialities of a lawyer's life is to be gathered from the biographies of those who have lived such a life and have revealed the relation of the legal profession to a life of deep satisfaction. I have in mind some such account of a career as that of Henry L. Stimson, as disclosed in Stimson and McBundy, *On Active Service.* But the most important thing for any generous and eager young spirit to remember is that any profession affords opportunities for a full life if pursued in the grand manner.

[1] *The Observer* (London), August 25, 1957, p. 5.

«« XI »»

Henry W. Edgerton

In honor of Judge Henry W. Edgerton's twentieth anniversary on the federal bench in 1957, the *Cornell Law Quarterly* 43:161 (Winter 1957) dedicated an issue to the work of its law school's former professor. Mr. Justice Frankfurter's contribution introduced the materials in the issue that was otherwise made up largely of Judge Edgerton's own writings.

"ALL LAW," wrote Lord Bryce, as quoted by Judge William S. Andrews, "is a compromise between the past and the present, between tradition and convenience." According to Dean Roscoe Pound, "All thinking about law has struggled to reconcile the conflicting demands of the need of stability and of the need of change." Sir Frederick Pollock entitled one of his most illuminating essays, "Judicial Caution and Valour." These three commanding legal thinkers have expressed in varying terms the problem that is at the core of judicial law-making and thereby indicated the subtle task that confronts a judge. Obviously, the most abstruse and delicate piercings of modern mathematics or of chemistry could not achieve a formula for an appropriate apportionment of the relevant components of valor and caution, stability and change, tradition and convenience, in the myriad of instances that solicit the judicial judgment.

The demands thus made are enormously enhanced wherever the judicial office historically derives from that of the English judge. For its conception is rooted in the ways and methods of empiricism, not only in the unfolding of law, case by case, but also in the seemingly happy-go-lucky mode of making judges: in the Anglo-American judicial world, unlike the Continental system, judges are not trained to be judges. This is only seemingly so regarding the English judiciary because the rather narrow, intimate circle which constitutes the English bar operates under conditions whereby normally lawyers are sent to the bench for proven judicial qualifications. But even with us, though we have not the sifting process afforded by the English situation, every once in a while a man becomes a judge who has been effectively trained for a judgeship in ways not unlike the training of men for a judicial career on the Continent. Judge Henry W. Edgerton is a striking illustration of the operation of such a felicitous if not formally designed training procedure. The range and depth of his academic experience and of his legal writings, and his awareness of the recalcitrances of practice and of government, singularly well prepared him for a judgeship. Especially was he prepared for the appellate tribunal so strategically related to the judicial scrutiny of the conduct of the national government as the Court of Appeals for the District of Columbia.

I venture to believe that the qualities which should be sought for in members of the Supreme Court are not less requisite for the court which Henry W. Edgerton graces. The first requisite is disinterestedness; the second requisite is disinterestedness; the third is disinterestedness. This means, in short, the habit of self-discipline so inured that merely personal views or passions are effectively antisepticized and thereby bar a corrosion of judgment leading to arbitrary determinations. This presupposes, in the language of the Massachusetts Declaration of Rights, "judges as free, impartial and independent as the lot of humanity will admit." These are, no doubt, severe exactions. But their essential fulfillment is required for a free society in which judges are entrusted with the powers given to them in this country.

The traditions of German scholarship have encouraged the happy practice of celebrating a notable anniversary in a learned man's life by a *Festschrift*. In taking note of Judge Edgerton's twenty years of distinguished judicial service, the *Cornell Law Quarterly* has done better, if I may say so, than to let others speak about him. The *Quarterly* is wisely letting Judge Edgerton's work, in all its variety and amplitude, speak for itself by significant samples. After all, that is the only way in which a judge can speak. Granted requisite qualities, it is the only way by which his work endures.

XII

The Supreme Court in the Mirror of Justices

Because of the mutuality of affection and respect between them, Mr. Justice Frankfurter was the appropriate choice to inaugurate the Owen J. Roberts Memorial Lectures at the University of Pennsylvania Law School on March 20, 1957. The lecture was first published in the *University of Pennsylvania Law Review* 105:781 (April 1957).

"Let us now praise famous men" was not an exhortation for a gesture of pietistic generosity, the placing of verbal flowers on the graves of famous men. It is for our sake that we are to praise them, for, as Ecclesiasticus added, they have given us an "inheritance." We commune with them to enlighten our understanding of the significance of life, to refine our faculties as assayers of values, to fortify our will in pursuing worthy ends. The qualities of mind and character of Owen Roberts and the uses to which he put them summon us to a better appreciation of the good life and a steadier devotion to it. This law school, which so proudly knew him as student, teacher, and dean, and from which he drew such strength throughout his life, fittingly commemorates him in the mode that would have pleased him most. And so, I am more deeply grateful than I can put into words for your generosity in allowing me to inagurate this Lectureship and to salute my friend and brother, Mr. Justice Roberts, howsoever inadequate the manner of doing it.

The last thing that Justice Roberts would want is that this lectureship should be turned into a laudatory exercise. Nothing would that exquisitely modest man deplore more. But in opening this Owen J. Roberts lecture series what is more natural than to turn our thoughts to the institution to which, by the very nature of the problems that are its concerns, he gave his deepest reflection. While Justice Roberts suggests my general theme, it has, for one in my place, almost forbidding difficulties. If I hug the shore of safety, I shall go very little beyond a snug harbor. If I set out as a privateer I would quickly be out of bounds, heedless of the course that it is my first duty to observe, above all to observe on an occasion dedicated to the example of Justice Roberts' character. I am temerarious enough to believe that I can clear the horns of this menacing dilemma. At all events, I shall attempt to escape offering you the jejune product of timid discretion and yet speak only of things this side of indiscretion. My justification for saying what I feel free to say rests on the observation of that least conventionally minded intellect in the Court's history, Mr. Justice Holmes, when he said, in a different context more than forty years ago what is equally applicable today, "at this time we need education in the obvious more than investigation of the obscure," or, may I add, disclosure of the private.

To so learned a legal audience, I need hardly confess that my title is a plagiarism. Unlike the author of the famous, or should I say notorious, *The Mirror of Justices*, I do not shrink from responsibility for what I have written, partly at least because I have labored to avoid his unreliability. And my motive, if I know it, is the antithesis of that thirteenth-century author, Andrew Horn, if it was Andrew Horn. He wrote to expose the judges of his day but also, romancer that he was, so Maitland tells us, to amuse his readers. My purpose is to attest my devotion to an institution for which I have a feeling akin to reverence and to do so, as becomes an old teacher, by contributing to whatever small extent to a better understanding of the nature of its functions and of the qualifications for their exercise.

During the one hundred and sixty-seven years since the day appointed for its first session, ninety Justices have sat on the Supreme Court. The number of men over so long a period would seem to be sufficient to afford some light on the kind of experience or qualifications that may be deemed appropriate for service on the Court. Indeed, the actualities about the men who were appointed to the Court may well be wiser guides than abstract notions about the kind of men who should be named. Of the ninety Justices I shall consider seventy-five, omitting contemporary and relatively recent occupants of the Court. And my concern is not with the substantive views of these Justices—neither their conception of the nature of the judicial process generally nor of that process in the specialized context of Supreme Court business. I am dealing with externally ascertainable factors. One of these has been intermittently urged and, in recent years, revived in an extreme form. I refer to the suggestion, indeed the assumption that, since the Supreme Court is the highest judicial tribunal, prior "judicial service" is not only a desirable, but an indispensable, qualification.

What is the teaching of history on this? Of the seventy-five Justices, twenty-eight had not a day's prior judicial service. Seven more had sat on some bench from a few months to not more than two years. Nine sat six years or less. Measures have been proposed that would require "judicial service" of not less than five years in a lower federal court or as a member of the highest court of a state;

some bills demand ten years of such service. A five-year requirement would have ruled out at least thirty-five of the seventy-five judges (in fact more, because several of the Justices who had had judicial experience did not sit on a federal bench or on the highest court of a state), and the ten-year requirement would have barred certainly forty-five of our seventy-five Justices.

Who were these Justices who came on the Supreme Court without any "judicial service," without even the judicial experience of an Iredell, who at the age of twenty-six sat on the Superior Court of his state, North Carolina, only long enough—six months—to resign.[1] They begin with your own James Wilson and include Bushrod Washington, Marshall, Story, Taney, Curtis, Campbell, Miller, Chase, Bradley, Waite, Fuller, Moody, Hughes, Brandeis, Stone, and Roberts. Of the twelve Chief Justices within our period, five had not had any judicial experience at the time of their appointment as Chief Justice and two more had had none when they first came on the Court.

Apart from the significance of a Chief Justice as the administrative head of the Court,[2] what of the quality of judicial service of the men who came on the Court totally devoid of judicial experience? Assessment of distinction in the realm of the mind and spirit cannot exclude subjective factors. Yet it is as true of judges as of poets or philosophers that whatever may be the fluctuations in what is called the verdict of history, varying and conflicting views finally come to rest and there arises a consensus of informed judgment. It would indeed be a surprising judgment that would exclude Marshall, William Johnson, Story, Taney,

[1] Griffith John McRee, *The Life and Correspondence of James Iredell* (New York, 1857), I, 367, 395.

[2] See statement by Mr. Justice Holmes in Willard Leroy King, *Melville Weston Fuller* (New York, 1950), pp. 334–335.

Miller, Field, Bradley, White (despite his question-begging verbosities), Holmes, Hughes, Brandeis, and Cardozo in the roster of distinction among our seventy-five. I myself would add Curtis, Campbell, Matthews, and Moody. (Some might prefer the first Harlan or Brewer or Brown.) Of the first twelve, five had had judicial experience and seven none before coming on the Court; of the others only Matthews can be counted a judge, for a brief period, before he came to Washington. Of the sixteen Justices whom I deem preeminent, only six came to the Court with previous judicial experience, however limited. It would require discernment more than daring, it would demand complete indifference to the elusive and intractable factors in tracking down causes, in short, it would be capricious, to attribute acknowledged greatness in the Court's history either to the fact that a Justice had had judicial experience or that he had been without it.

Greatness in the law is not a standardized quality, nor are the elements that combine to attain it. To speak only of Justices near enough to one's own time, greatness may manifest itself through the power of penetrating analysis exerted by a trenchant mind, as in the case of Bradley; it may be due to persistence in a point of view forcefully expressed over a long judicial stretch, as shown by Field; it may derive from a coherent judicial philosophy, expressed with pungency and brilliance, reinforced by the *Zeitgeist*, which in good part was itself a reflection of that philosophy, as was true of Holmes; it may be achieved by the resourceful deployment of vast experience and an originating mind, as illustrated by Brandeis; it may result from the influence of a singularly endearing personality in the service of sweet reason, as Cardozo proves; it may come through the kind of vigor that exerts moral authority over others, as embodied in Hughes.

The roll call of preeminent members of the Supreme Court who had had no judicial experience in itself establishes, one would suppose, that judicial experience is not a prerequisite for that Court. It would be hard to gainsay that this galaxy outshines even the distinguished group that came to the Court with prior experience on state courts, though these judges included the great names of Holmes and Cardozo. It has been suggested that the appearance on the Court of Marshall, Story, Taney, Curtis, Campbell, Miller, Bradley, Hughes, and Brandeis, all without prior judicial experience, is "a curious accident." But this accident has been thrown up by history over a period of one hundred and fifty years. After all, these men were not self-appointed. They must have been found by, or suggested to, the various and very different Presidents who named them. In at least one instance a lawyer without prior judicial experience was urged on a President by the Court itself—John A Campbell, whose prior judicial experience was his refusal, twice, to go on the Supreme Court of Alabama.[3] (It would indeed be interesting to ascertain what men were recommended for appointment when the Executive invited suggestions from the Court.)

The notion that prior judicial experience is a prerequisite for the Supreme Court, whether made a formal statutory requirement or acted upon as an accepted assumption, deserves closer scrutiny than its *ad hominem* refutation. Apart from meaning that a man had sat on some court for some time, "judicial service" tells nothing that is relevant about the qualifications for the functions exercised by the Supreme Court. While it seems to carry meaning, it misleads. To an uncritical mind it carries emanations of relevance in that it implies that a man who sat on a lower court has qualifications for sitting on a higher court, or, con-

[3] Henry Groves Connor, *John A. Campbell* (Boston and New York, 1920), pp. 16–17; 20 Wall. ix (1873).

versely, that a man has not the qualifications for sitting on a higher court unless he has had the experience of having sat on a lower court, just as a man presumably cannot run a mile in less than four minutes unless he had already run it in six, or a player has not the aptitude or experience for a major league unless he has played in a minor league.

Need I say that judicial experience is not like that at all? For someone to have been a judge on some court for some time, having some kind of business resulting in some kind of experience, may have some abstract relation to the Supreme Court conceived of as an abstract judicial tribunal. The Supreme Court is a very special kind of court. "Judicial service" as such has no significant relation to the kinds of litigation that come before the Supreme Court, to the types of issues they raise, to qualities that these actualities require for wise decision.

To begin with, one must consider the differences in the staple business of different courts and the different experiences to which different judicial business gives rise, and the bearing of different experiences so generated on the demands of the business of the Supreme Court. Thus, there is a vital difference, so far as substantive training is afforded, between the experience gained on state courts and on the lower federal courts. There are the so-called federal specialties whose importance for the Supreme Court has copiously receded since the Evarts Act of 1891,[4] but is still relevant to its work. One would suppose that if prior judicial experience would especially commend itself for Supreme Court appointments, the federal courts would furnish most materials for promotion. History falsifies such expectation. Of the forty-seven Justices who had had some kind of prior judicial experience, no matter how short, fifteen came from the federal courts—Trimble, Barbour,

4 Act of March 3, 1891, c. 517, 26 Stat. 826 (codified in scattered sections of 28 U.S.C.).

Daniel, Woods, Blatchford, Brewer, Brown, Howell E. Jackson, McKenna, Day, Lurton, Taft, Sanford, Van Devanter, and John H. Clarke—whereas thirty-two had only experience on state courts.

How meagerly the experience on a state court, even if of long duration, prepares one for work on the Supreme Court is strikingly borne out by the testimony of the two Justices who are indubitably the two most outstanding of those who came to the Supreme Court from State courts. After having spent twenty years on the Supreme Judicial Court of Massachusetts, part of it as Chief Justice, in the course of which he wrote more than a thousand opinions on every conceivable subject, Mr. Justice Holmes found himself not at all at home on coming to the Supreme Court. Listen to what he wrote to his friend Pollock after a month in his new judicial habitat:

> Yes—here I am—and more absorbed, interested and impressed than ever I had dreamed I might be. The work of the past seems a finished book—locked up far away, and a new and solemn volume opens. The variety and novelty to me of the questions, the remote spaces from which they come, the amount of work they require, all help the effect. I have written on the constitutionality of part of the Constitution of California, on the powers of the Railroad Commissioners of Arkansas, on the question whether a law of Wisconsin impairs the obligation of the plaintiff's contract. I have to consider a question between a grant of the U.S. in aid of a military road and an Indian reservation on the Pacific coast. I have heard conflicting mining claims in Arizona and whether a granite quarry is "Minerals" within an exception in a Railway land grant and fifty other things as remote from each other as these.[5]

Nor did Cardozo, after eighteen years on the New York Court of Appeals, five of them as Chief Judge, in the course

[5] Mark DeWolfe Howe, ed., *The Holmes-Pollock Letters: The Correspondence of Mr. Justice Holmes and Sir Frederick Pollock, 1874–1935*, 2 vols. (Cambridge, Mass., 1941), I, 109–110.

of which he gained the acclaim of the whole common-law world, find that his transplantation from Albany to Washington was a natural step in judicial progression. On more than one occasion he complained to friends (sometimes as bitterly as that gentle soul could) that he should not have been taken from judicial labors with which he was familiar and which were congenial to him, to types of controversies to which his past experience bore little relation and to which, though these were the main concern of the Supreme Court, he was not especially drawn.

To be sure, by the time that Holmes and Cardozo came to the Supreme Bench, the heavy stream of commercial and common-law litigation that reached the Supreme Court in its earlier periods had been diverted to the courts of appeals and largely stopped there. But even when a good deal of the business of the Court consisted of litigation related to what loosely may be called common-law litigation, the transition from a state court to the Supreme Court was not in a straight line of experience. Thus, although on the bench in Connecticut Ellsworth's opinions sustained "his reputation as a good lawyer and a just and able judge"[6] and in the Senate he had been the chief architect of the First Judiciary Act, on his appointment by Washington as Chief Justice, he "undertook a severe course of study and reading."[7] And when Monroe offered a place on the Court to his Secretary of the Navy, Smith Thompson, who had been a New York judge for seventeen years and for nearly five Kent's successor as Chief Justice, Thompson hesitated to accept, in part because of his lack of judicial experience outside the common law.[8]

6 William Garrott Brown, *The Life of Oliver Ellsworth* (New York and London, 1905), p. 109.

7 *Ibid.*, p. 242.

8 *Dictionary of American Biography*, vol. XVIII (New York, 1936), p. 472.

But, it may be suggested, if experience on a state court does not adequately prepare even the greatest of judges for the problems that are the main and certainly the most important business of the Supreme Court, judicial experience intrinsically fosters certain habits of mind and attitudes, serves to train the faculties of detachment, begets habits of aloofness from daily influences, in short, educates and reinforces those moral qualities—disinterestedness and deep humility—which are indeed preconditions for the wise exercise of the judicial function on the Supreme Bench. Unhappily, history again disappoints such expectation. What is more inimical for good work on the Court than for a Justice to cherish political, and more particularly Presidential, ambition? Who will disagree with Mr. Justice Holmes's observation, "I think a judge should extinguish such thoughts when he goes on the Bench."[9] Sad and strange as it may be, the most numerous and in many ways the worst offenders in this regard have been men who came to the Court from state courts, in some instances with long service on such courts. Their temperamental partisanship and ambition were stronger than the disciplining sway supposedly exercised by the judiciary. To be sure, there have been instances of such political ambition by those who came on the Court without judicial experience. Salmon P. Chase, of course, is a conspicuous example. But I think it is fair to say that fewer Justices who had had no prior judicial experience dallied with political ambition while on the Court than those who came there with it. And it deserves to be noted that the most vigorous, indeed aggressive hostility to availability of a member of the Court for a Presidential nomination came from one who had no prior judicial experience, Chief Justice Waite,[10] and from an-

[9] *The Holmes-Pollock Letters*, I, 192.

[10] Bruce Raymond Trimble, *Chief Justice Waite: Defender of the Public Interest* (London, 1938), p. 141.

other whose name ought not to go unmentioned on this occasion—Mr. Justice Roberts.

Even though the history of the Court may demonstrate that judicial experience whether on state or federal bench ought not to be deemed a prerequisite, what of the lower courts as a training ground for the Supreme Bench? The fact is that not one so trained emerges over a century and a half among the few towering figures of the Court. Oblivion has overtaken almost all of them. Probably the most intellectually powerful of the lot, Mr. Justice Brewer, does not owe the weight of the strength that he exerted on the Court to his five years on the circuit court after his long service on Kansas courts. Surely it is safe to attribute it to the native endowment that the famous Field strain gave him. Mr. Justice Van Devanter was undoubtedly a very influential member of the so-called Taft Court. But he was that essentially on the procedural aspect of the Court's business and by virtue of the extent to which Chief Justice Taft leaned on him. It was characteristic of Taft's genial candor that he spoke of Van Devanter outside the purlieus of the Supreme Court as "my chancellor."

One is not unappreciative of Chief Justice Taft by saying that his significance in the Court's history is not that of an intellectual leader but as the effective force in modernizing the federal judiciary and in promoting jurisdictional changes to enable the Court to be capable of discharging its role in our federal scheme. Moreover, it was not Taft's eight years of service on the Sixth Circuit, highly esteemed as it was, that led President Harding to make him Chief Justice White's successor after Taft's twenty years of separation from active concern with law. Taft's situation reminds of the Hamilton Fish incident. That very able man declined President Grant's offer of the Chief Justiceship, believing that his knowledge of the law had become stale and his feeling for it rusty, having for long been unexercised. "I insisted that I could not accept it; that it was upwards of twenty years since I had had any connection with the bar or practice, and I had no familiarity now with the proceedings of the courts. . . ."[11] It was of course true of Fish as it was of Taft that his unusual experience in public affairs informed his understanding, even if not in their legal aspects, of problems that reach the Supreme Court. But in Taft's case, after his political career was over, he must have renewed his familiarity with legal problems as Kent Professor at the Yale Law School, light as were his duties there.

More immediately relevant to our subject is the fact that even Justices who have come to the Supreme Court fresh from a longish and conspicuously competent tenure on the lower federal courts do not find the demands of their new task familiar. Their lower court experience does not make the transition an easy one. Thus Philip Barbour, despite the deserved reputation that he brought to the Supreme Court from his years on the United States district court, felt it necessary to fit himself by "conscientious study" for his duties on the Supreme Court.[12] A recent striking example of how hard the sledding can be for a judge who also made an exceptional record over long years on the district court and was an uncommonly cultivated man, was Mr. Justice Sanford. Thus it has been as true of capable Justices who came to Washington from lower federal courts as of those who came to the Court richly endowed but without judicial experience, that they actively set about educating themselves for the work of the Court and were educated by it.

Mr. Justice Moody, who had had exceptional preparation for the Court's work as lawyer, legislator, and member of the Cabinet, including forensic activity as Attorney

[11] Allen Nevins, *Hamilton Fish* (New York, 1936), p. 661.

[12] *Dictionary of American Biography*, vol. I (New York, 1928), p. 596.

General, on his appointment to the Court turned to his classmate, Professor Eugene Wambaugh of the Harvard Law School, for guidance in the study of constitutional law and the jurisdiction of the Supreme Court as eagerly as any avid neophyte. Again, Mr. Justice Brandeis who brought not only as well-stocked a mind for the substantive issues with which he had to deal as a Justice as any member of the Court but also a reputation second to none as an advocate before it, used to say that no one can have the right kind of feel regarding the distinctive jurisdictional and procedural problems touching the Court's business in less than three or four terms of actual service on the Court. He set about to acquire mastery of this essential aspect of the Court's business by studying the *Reports*, from Dallas down. Nor did he limit his systematic study of the Court's business to these aspects. Thus, he spent one whole summer in familiarizing himself with all the decisions of the Court pertaining to criminal law. These modern instances are recognition of the truth discerned from the beginning of the Court, that membership on it involves functions and calls for faculties as different from those called for by other judicial positions as those called for by private practice or nonjudicial service.

In response to an inquiry by the House of Representatives into the federal judicial system that had just been set up, Attorney General Edmund Randolph, addressing himself more particularly to the undesirability of the circuit duties with which the Justices were charged, wrote the following:[13]

> Those who pronounce the law of the land without appeal, ought to be pre-eminent in most endowments of the mind. Survey the functions of a judge of the Supreme Court. He

[13] 1 American State Papers 23–24 (1834) (report of the Attorney General on the judiciary system, read in the House of Representatives, December 31, 1790).

must be a master of the common law in all its divisions, a chancellor, a civilian, a federal jurist, and skilled in the laws of each State. To expect that in future times this assemblage of talents will be ready, without further study, for the national service, is to confide too largely in the public fortune. Most vacancies on the bench will be supplied by professional men, who, perhaps, have been too much animated by the contentions of the bar deliberately to explore this extensive range of science. In a great measure, then, the supreme judges will form themselves after their nomination. But what leisure remains from their itinerant dispensation of justice? Sum up all the fragments of their time, hold their fatigue at naught, and let them bid adieu to all domestic concerns, still the average term of a life, already advanced, will be too short for any important proficiency.

Circuit-riding ceased long before members of the Court were statutorily relieved of it, and the establishment of the circuit courts of appeals in 1891 freed the Court of the vast mass of what roughly may be called private litigation that used to come to it by way of diversity jurisdiction and the federal specialties. And the Judiciary Act of 1925[14] has made the Court the master of its docket so that it now may be free to concern itself only with cases that have a substantial public interest. Yet it is still true today as it was when Randolph wrote in 1790 that "in a great measure . . . the supreme judges will form themselves after their nomination." This is true as we have seen even of men in the highest capacity, men who had had wide professional experience with the federal courts before they came on the Supreme Court as well as of judges with long service on the federal bench.

In addition to all other considerations, this is so because the practical workings of the Supreme Court, not only in our governmental scheme but in the influences it exerts on

14 Act of Feb. 13, 1925, c. 229, §237, 43 Stat. 937.

our national life, to no small extent are determined by the effective administration of the appellate jurisdiction allotted to the Court, the manner in which it conceives what issues are open on review, and how it deals with them—raising not only unique problems in the wise articulation of its jurisdiction with that of the lower federal courts and the state courts but often involving perplexities in the successful operation of our federal system. These are subtle matters carrying deep implications that do not lie on the surface. Partly because of their seemingly technical nature and partly because they have few dramatic ingredients, they are hardly appreciated by the laity and all too little by the profession at large. The proper treatment of these problems has far-reaching consequences, but they do not bulk big in the work of lower courts and therefore do not become part of the experience of judges either on the state courts or on the lower federal courts.

Not only is the framework within which the judicial process of the Supreme Court operates drastically different from the jurisdictional and procedural concern of other courts but the cases that now come before the Court, and will increasingly in the future, present issues that make irrelevant considerations in the choice of Justices that at former periods had pertinence. Mastery of the federal specialties by some members of the Court was an obvious need of the Court in days when a substantial part of the Court's business related to such specialties. Thus, when maritime and patent cases appeared frequently enough on the Court's docket, it was highly desirable to have a judge so experienced in these fields as was Judge Blatchford when he was named to the Court. The extent of the Court's maritime litigation naturally brought Henry Billings Brown, an outstanding admiralty judge, to the Court. And since the business that came to the Court in times past reflected to no small degree sectionally different economic interests, geographic considerations had their relevance. Thus, when the western circuit, consisting of Ohio, Kentucky, and Tennessee, was established, at a time when litigation dealing with land title and other local property questions was important, the selection of one conversant with these problems was clearly indicated. Therefore, on the recommendation of the representatives in Congress from the interested states, Jefferson named Thomas Todd, the then Chief Justice of the Kentucky Court of Appeals. Still later, when California opened up not only a new world for gold-rushers but also a new world of litigation for the Supreme Court, it was inevitable that a judge as knowledgeable about western land and mineral law as was Stephen J. Field should be named to the Court.

All this has changed. Not only in the course of a hundred years but in the course of fifty years. Today there is a totally different flow of business to the Court from what it was a hundred years ago; it is predominantly different from what it was fifty years ago.

An examination of the *Reports* in these three periods demonstrates the great changes that have taken place. Analysis of the written opinions of the Court a hundred years ago, in the 1854 and 1855 Terms (17 and 18 How.) discloses that, aside from questions of Supreme Court practice and procedure, four major categories of litigation, comprising two-thirds of the cases decided by written opinion, occupied the Court's time. The four categories were (1) estates and trusts, (2) admiralty, (3) real property, and (4) contracts and commercial law. With one partial exception, common-law questions comprised the major categories of the litigation coming before the Court. The exception is that perhaps one-third to one-half of the real property cases involved, directly or indirectly, questions of federal land law. The remaining third of the litigation that occupied the Court one hundred years ago involved a variety of issues: a number of constitutional cases, a few patent, tariff, corporation, tort, and bankruptcy cases, and the rest scattered.

Fifty years later, in the 1904 and 1905 terms (195–203 U.S.), not only had the volume of the Court's work increased greatly but its nature had changed considerably, especially because of the fourteenth amendment, the Judiciary Act of 1875,[15] and the Circuit Court of Appeals Act of 1891.[16] Constitutional law had become by far the major item of the Court's business, involving approximately one-third of the cases decided by written opinion. And questions under the fourteenth amendment comprised one-half of all the constitutional cases. These apart, the Court's business was almost equally divided between questions of public and private law. Real property law was the next largest class of cases after constitutional law, with federal land law comprising almost the entire category. The remaining principal types of litigation included federal jurisdiction, bankruptcy, corporations, estates and trusts, commercial law and contracts, and torts. Admiralty litigation, which had formed a major portion of the Court's work fifty years previous, was negligible. Significant as indicating the increasing industrialization of the country was the dual increase in corporate and tort law cases. Significant also for the number of pages in the *Reports* and perhaps also as a portent for the future were several antitrust and Interstate Commerce Commission cases.

Examination of the work of the two most recent terms (348–351 U.S.) indicates how complete the reversal of the

[15] Act of March 3, 1875, c. 137, 18 Stat. 470.

[16] Act of March 3, 1891, c. 517, 26 Stat. 826 (codified in scattered sections of 28 U.S.C.).

character of the Supreme Court's business has been. Whereas a hundred years ago, private common-law litigation represented the major part of the Court's business, and fifty years ago, constitutional cases apart, public and private law business was equally divided, today private litigation has become virtually negligible. Constitutional law and cases with constitutional undertones are of course still very important, with almost one-fourth of the cases in which written opinions were filed involving such questions. Review of administrative action, mainly reflecting enforcement of federal regulatory statutes, constitutes the largest category of the Court's work, comprising one-third of the total cases decided on the merits. The remaining significant categories of litigation—federal criminal law, federal jurisdiction, immigration and nationality law, federal taxation—all involve largely public-law questions.

The Court was of course from the beginning the interpreter of the Constitution and thereby, for all practical purposes, the adjuster of governmental powers in our complicated federal sytem. But the summary of the contemporaneous business before the Court that is reflected in written opinions statistically establishes these constitutional adjudications and kindred public-law issues as constituting almost the whole of Supreme Court litigation. It is essentially accurate to say that the Court's preoccupation today is with the application of rather fundamental aspirations and what Judge Learned Hand calls "moods," embodied in provisions like the due process and equal protection clauses, which were designed not to be precise and positive directions for rules of action. The judicial process in applying them involves a judgment on the processes of government. The Court sits in judgment, that is, on the views of the direct representatives of the people in meeting the needs of society, on the views of Presidents and Governors, and by their construction of the will of legislatures the Court breathes life, feeble or strong, into the inert pages of the Constitution and the statute books.

Such functions surely call for capacious minds and reliable powers for disinterested and fair-minded judgment. It demands the habit of curbing any tendency to reach results agreeable to desire or to embrace the solution of a problem before exhausting its comprehensive analysis. One in whose keeping may be the decision of the Court must have a disposition to be detached and withdrawn. To be sure, these moral qualities, for such they are, are desirable in all judges, but they are indispensable for the Supreme Court. Its task is to seize the permanent, more or less, from the feelings and fluctuations of the transient. Therefore it demands the kind of equipment that Doctor Johnson rather grandiloquently called "genius," namely, "a mind of large general powers accidentally determined to some particular direction as against particular designation of mind and propensity for some essential employment."

For those wielding ultimate power it is easy to be either willful or wooden: willful, in the sense of enforcing individual views instead of speaking humbly as the voice of law by which society presumably consents to be ruled, without too much fiction in attributing such consent; wooden, in uncritically resting on formulas, in assuming the familiar to be the necessary, in not realizing that any problem can be solved if only one principle is involved but that unfortunately all controversies of importance involve if not a conflict at least an interplay of principles.

If these commonplaces regarding the reach of the powers of the Supreme Court and the majesty of the functions entrusted to nine mere mortals give anyone the impression that a Justice of the Court is left at large to exercise his private wisdom, let me hasten to say as quickly and as emphatically as I can that no one could possibly be more hostile to such a notion than I am. These men are judges, bound by the restrictions of the judicial function, and all the more so bound because the nature of the controversies that they adjudicate inevitably leaves more scope for insight, imagination, and prophetic responsibility than the types of litigation that come before other courts. It was the least mentally musclebound and the most creative mind among Justices, Mr. Justice Holmes, who, with characteristic pithiness, described his task as "that of solving a problem according to the rules by which one is bound."[17] Some years later, Chief Justice Hughes spelled out Holmes's thought. "We do not write on a blank sheet. The Court has its jurisprudence, the helpful repository of the deliberate and expressed convictions of generations of sincere minds addressing themselves to exposition and decision, not with the freedom of casual critics or even of studious commentators, but under the pressure and within the limits of a definite official responsibility."[18]

This is not abstract or self-deceiving talk. The great men in the Court's history give proof of its truth. Will anyone deny that the four most distinguished minds of the latter part of the period under review were Holmes, Hughes, Brandeis, and Cardozo? All four had the largeness of view so essential for adjudicating the great issues before the Court. But is it just a coincidence that all four were to a superlative degree technically equipped lawyers? They built on that equipment for the larger tasks of the Court; they were not confined by it. Again, is it mere coincidence that all four were widely read and deeply cultivated men whose reading and cultivation gave breadth and depth to

[17] *Speeches by Oliver Wendell Holmes* (Boston, 1934), p. 99.

[18] 309 U.S. xiv (1940). (Statement by Chief Justice Hughes on the occasion of the 150th anniversary of the Court).

their understanding of legal problems and infused their opinions?

I have now come to the end of my story with its self-evident moral. Since the functions of the Supreme Court are what they are and demand the intellectual and moral qualities that they do, inevitably touching interests not less than those of the nation, does it require an explicit statement that in choosing men for this task no artificial or irrelevant consideration should restrict choice?

The search should be made among those men, inevitably very few at any time, who gave the best promise of satisfying the intrinsic needs of the Court, no matter where they may be found, no matter in what professional way they have manifested the needed qualities. Of course these needs do not exclude prior judicial experience, but, no less surely, they do not call for judicial experience. One is entitled to say without qualification that the correlation between prior judicial experience and fitness for the functions of the Supreme Court is zero. The significance of the greatest among the Justices who had had such experience, Holmes and Cardozo, derived not from that judicial experience but from the fact that they were Holmes and Cardozo. They were thinkers, and more particularly legal philosophers. The seminal ideas of Holmes, by which to so large an extent he changed the whole atmosphere of legal thinking, were formulated by him before he ever was a judge in Massachusetts. And while the Court of Appeals gave Cardozo an opportunity to express his ideas in opinions, Cardozo was Cardozo before he became a judge. On the other side, Bradley and Brandeis had the preeminent qualities they had and brought to the Court, without any training that judicial experience could have given them.

There is another irrelevance, regard for which may lead to a narrower choice than that to which the country is entitled—geographic considerations. The claims of uncritical tradition led President Hoover, who had the most impressive recommendations for naming Cardozo as Holmes's successor, to hesitate because there were at the time already two New Yorkers on the Court. When the President urged this difficulty on Senator Borah, the latter, to the President's astonishment, said that Cardozo was no New Yorker. When asked to explain, the Senator replied that Cardozo belonged as much to Idaho as to New York. Those of sufficient stature for the Court in its modern responsibilities should not be sought among men who have professionally a merely parochial significance and choice of them should not be restricted to a confined area. From the point of view of intrinsic need, any geographical consideration has long since become irrelevant. The pride of a region in having one of its own on the Court does not outweigh the loss to the Court and the country in so narrowing the search for the most qualified.

Perhaps a word should be said on the bearing of political affiliations that men had before coming on the Court to their work on it. The fact is that past party ties as such tell next to nothing about future Justices. The Democratic President Wilson put two Democrats from the bar on the Court; but what notions about law and life, about their conception of their functions as Justices, did James C. McReynolds and Louis D. Brandeis share? President Harding was commended for his broad-mindedness in selecting the Democrat Pierce Butler for the Court[19] at the time that he named his former Republican senatorial colleague, George Sutherland, a Justice much cherished by brethren most in disagreement with him. It would not be inaccurate to say that Butler, the Democrat, and Sutherland, the Re-

[19] For a vivid delineation of this strong-minded judge, see 310 U.S. xiii (1940) (address by Attorney General Jackson to the Court).

publican, were judicial twins. But when Harlan F. Stone came on the Court, the stout Republicanism that Sutherland and Stone had shared was not at all reflected in a shared outlook as Justices. A matter that is kindred to looking for party ties as an index to the behavior of future Justices is the expectation of Presidents regarding the outlook of their appointees on matters of great moment that may come before the Court. There can be little doubt that Lincoln would have been as surprised and perhaps as displeased by his Secretary of the Treasury's attitude toward the Legal Tender Act, when Chase, as Chief Justice, passed on its constitutionality,[20] as was President Theodore Roosevelt by Holmes's dissent in the *Northern Securities* case.[21] The upshot of the matter is that only by disregard of all these irrelevancies in the appointment of Justices will the Court adequately meet its august responsibilities.

Selection wholly on the basis of functional fitness not only affords the greatest assurance that the Court will best fulfill its functions. It also will, by the quality of such performance, most solidly establish the Court in the confidence of the people, and the confidence of the people is the ultimate reliance of the Court as an institution.

20 Legal Tender Cases, 79 U.S. (12 Wall.) 457, 570 (1870) (dissenting opinion).

21 Northern Securities Co. v. United States, 193 U.S. 197, 400 (1904).

XIII

Jerome N. Frank

Jerome N. Frank (1889–1957) came to the bench of the Court of Appeals for the Second Circuit after a distinguished career at the bar and in the administrative agencies of the national government, including the post of Chairman of the Securities and Exchange Commission. He was a leader in the movement — it cannot be called a school — for realistic jurisprudence. His most important work in this regard was his early book *Law and the Modern Mind* (1930). As in the case of almost anyone who held important posts in the New Deal, he was an intimate of Mr. Justice Frankfurter who shared some of the responsibility for bringing him to Washington in the first place. These memorial remarks of the Justice were published in the *University of Chicago Law Review* 24:625 (Spring 1957).

Some authors, including judges, are less than their writings, some more. To have known Jerome Frank only through his writings was not to have known him. On paper he appeared prickly and pugilistic; in personal relations he was warm-hearted and generous. His combative curiosity gave battle at the drop of a word, so that those who encountered him only on paper were apt to be surprised when they found in him a devoted, uncritical friend and a compassionate observer of the human scene. His insatiable desire to understand was his dominant impulse as a writer both before he went on the bench and as a judge. No judge in our time used his judicial opinions so systematically as a candid and discursive means for legal education. Needless to say, he was a great believer in adult education; he employed it most vigorously in his own behalf. While he somehow managed to envelop himself in an atmosphere of dogmatism, he was singularly free of bias or imprisoning doctrine. His seeming iconoclasm was rooted in his zealous loyalty to the realization that the history of thought, particularly sociological thought, is the history of continuous displacement of erroneous dogma.

Contributions to thought are not to be determined by the actual increase to the body of knowledge. Men may greatly further the thinking of others even though their own ideas be rejected. There can be no doubt that Judge Frank served as a powerful ferment in formulating more searchingly the problems that are put to law and in discouraging distortion of such problems by question-begging and parochial answers. It must be left to others to do justice to the juristic contributions of this unflagging pursuer of understanding. The melancholy purpose of these inadequate words is to say farewell to a much-cherished friend, an ardent seeker after truth and justice.

XIV

Maurice Finkelstein

Maurice Finkelstein (1899–1957) was one of many of Mr. Justice Frankfurter's students who spent his life teaching law. The issue of the *St. John's Law Review* 31:244 (May 1957), dedicated to that school's long-time teacher, began with these comments by the Justice.

DURING the academic year 1922–1923 Maurice Finkelstein was one of a group of unusually able and attractive men who were in a seminar of mine at the Harvard Law School. Perhaps the most compact way of conveying the impression he then left with me is to say that the sense of him after thirty-five years is as vivid and charming a personality as I then felt him to be, although we had not seen one another for years. The promise he gave in that seminar of a strong and urbane mind he vindicated in the years to follow. Very early he made a real contribution to as important inquiries as any that test legal scholarship, namely those that concern the nature of the judicial process and more particularly the demands of so-called issues of public law upon that process. (See Finkelstein, *Judicial Self-Limitation*, 37 Harv. L. Rev. 338 [1924]; *Further Notes on Judicial Self-Limitation*, 39 Harv. L. Rev. 221 [1925]).

Through occasional reprints from him and as I scanned the law reviews over the years, I could not but become aware of Finkelstein's scholarly fecundity. But not until

I made a systematic examination of his writings did I fully appreciate the range and depth of his output as a legal scholar. He brought clarity to recondite problems arising under the New York Law of Perpetuities and kept within the actualities when moving in what Dean Ezra Thayer facetiously called the higher realms of constitutional law. He was as well aware as anyone that legal problems reflect, consciously or unwittingly, philosophic and psychologic judgments, but he did not solve difficulties in the law by assuming answers to even more difficult intellectual problems outside the technical aspects of law. Even apart from his series of five case histories, his writings added not a little to understanding of the actual process of litigation through the courts.

Book-reviewing constitutes one of the most important aspects of legal literature, and Finkelstein's book reviews were notable. They were not extracted from the books reviewed but out of his well-stocked mind. His judgments were generous but critical, not namby-pamby, and always in the best of manner.

He left us much too early. But he leaves behind the cherished memory of a charming personality, a devoted friend, a fruitful scholar, a man of gifts and character who used them bountifully.

XV

Lord Percy of Newcastle

No American has been a greater Anglophile than Felix Frankfurter. It is not possible to say whether this was the cause or result of his multitudinous friendships with Englishmen, particularly those connected with the government and academic life. Lord Percy of Newcastle (1887–1958) was both a diplomat and educator. The Justice's friendship with Eustace Percy dates back to Percy's service in Washington on the staff of Lord Bryce when he was ambassador to the United States. From 1937 to 1952, Percy, who was the seventh son of the seventh Duke of Northumberland, was rector of the Newcastle Division of the University of Durham. Before that he had served in Parliament from 1921 to 1937, during which time he held several important posts in the government, including that of President of the Board of Education from 1924 to 1929. The following letter was published in *The Times* (London) on April 14, 1958 under the heading "American Friendships."

If it be true that the convergence in policies of the British Commonwealth and the United States has been greatly advanced by the propitious development through personal relations of the forces calculated to knit the two English-speaking peoples together, Eustace Percy was an important figure in this process. He illustrates the fact that deep and abiding influences among nations may be exerted in simpler and subtler ways than through the actions and arrangements of statesmen. Percy's life gives point and meaning to the loose talk about dealing with difficult international problems between people and people. During the last fifty years there can hardly have been a Britisher who sowed more seeds of appreciation and therefore of understanding between our two peoples. Especially is this true of the decade 1910–1920 when he served as a junior member of the Bryce Embassy and later of the Balfour Mission. And all this is not through his official work, important as that was. He had a considerable share in the successful negotiations with the Wilson Administration for abrogation of the discriminatory Panama Canal tolls, and he did as much as any of the able group who came with Lord Balfour to take the American Government to school in the conduct of a world war.

The significance of Percy lay in his connections with a multifarious body of influential Americans. Bryce and his more recent successors traveled widely over the United States and through their personal associations no doubt deepened a realization of the harmony of interests between the two nations, so vital to the well-being of the world. But probably not one of them acquired such a variegated collection of American friends as did Percy: Victor Berger, the Socialist Congressman from Wisconsin and William E. Borah, the Republican leader in the United States Senate; Ruth Hanna, the representative offspring of Mark Hanna, and Dr. Alice Hamilton, the associate of Jane Adams; Medill McCormick, of the *Chicago Tribune*, and Herbert Croly, the founder of *The New Republic;* Theodore Roosevelt and Louis D. Brandeis. Percy had friends by the score who were as different in outlook and interests as were these men and women.

One who saw Percy both on his native soil and in the United States could not but be struck by the extent to which the spontaneity and warmth of his nature were released on crossing the ocean. The United States seemed to tap a deep democratic strain in him. Freed, apparently, from all sorts of institutional inhibitions at home, his receptive and tender nature luxuriated in America. Since there was nothing shallow about him, his intimacies endured. Happily, he was able to keep his American friendships in repair until the outbreak of the second World War. Thereafter correspondence and American visits to England kept them flourishing. At least to one old friend he appeared to be at his happiest after he gave up politics to settle in his beloved Northumbria and heed the deep call of his nature as Rector of the Newcastle Division of the University of Durham.

There must be many Americans who bid him affectionate farewell.

XVI

The Morris Cohen Library

Mr. Justice Frankfurter's close friendship with the eminent philosopher Morris R. Cohen (1880–1947) began when both were students at Harvard, the one at the Law School, and the other in the Department of Philosophy studying for his doctorate. When the City College of New York, the *alma mater* of both, dedicated its new library to its most eminent professor, the Justice was the principal speaker at the dedication ceremonies on May 3, 1958.

FOR ME, this is a prized opportunity to say, however inadequately, my word of homage to four of my deepest loyalties in life.

The first is our city. I say *our* city, for such it has been and such it will remain, although I've wandered from it for most of the years of my life. It is my city because, when as a lad of twelve I sailed into the harbor of New York past the Statue of Liberty, it was as the soil of the city was touched that there began the noble and happy dream that is America. And when as a lad in Public School 25, without knowledge of the English language, I eventually understood the pledge to the flag—"I pledge allegiance to the flag of the United States of America and to the republic for which it stands, one nation, indivisible, with liberty and justice for all"—the words thrilled me then as they thrill me now.

It is said that New York is the least representative city of America. This is a shallow view. To me it is the most representative symbol of America, precisely because of the polyglot and multifarious forms of human life on this island, precisely because of the occasional dissonances in the life of this city, precisely because of the admixture of races, of views, of religions, of the lack of religions, of ethical allegiances, of rational developments. It is precisely because in this city we have that admixture of these forces in all their multitudinous variety that it constitutes the essence of the United States. And so when I come back as a wandering citizen of New York, I avow anew my deep feeling for what New York means as a symbol of America. Moreover, it is the city that has made possible the opportunity to attend a free college as the culmination of public education in a civilized society.

My second devotion is The City College. The College has given me not what I know—that isn't the point of education. (Someone once defined culture as the deposit of things forgotten.) But it has given me habits of thought, a sense of seriousness about intellectual issues, and a sense of responsibility as a citizen. To whatever meager extent I have been faithful to this heritage, I am indebted to The City College of New York.

Like all old graduates, I have a romantic feeling about what I suppose was an ugly building, that Gothic building on Lexington Avenue and 23rd Street. But it wasn't ugly to me. What was beautiful about it was not the things seen by the eye or capable of touch, but the kind of outlook on life, the habits of mind, the purposes which it engendered and which I have every right to believe this College, in its more spacious and opulent circumstances, still engenders.

This brings me to the third deep loyalty relevant to this occasion—the man whose name this marvelously beautiful and utilitarian building is to bear. Before we became roommates, Morris Cohen and I were friends. Two years is apt to be a big gulf in the life of collegiate generations. But somehow or other we had many friends in common. This helped to bridge the gulf. And so it was not unnatural for us to be roommates while he was trying to be a philosopher and I was trying to acquire some knowledge of the law.

Morris Cohen was a great teacher. Greatness in teaching is as rare as greatness in any other activity of man. Indeed greatness is ever so much rarer than the occasions on which it is used to describe people. Greatness in a teacher is, I suspect, as rare as greatness in a poet, greatness in a musician, greatness in the arts. What made him a great teacher? Though professional philosophers may say I am wrong, it is my impression that Morris Cohen was not original as the founder of a new metaphysic, as the formulator of a novel philosophic system. But about this, I am not entitled to an opinion.

I am not suggesting that he was not an original man. He was a highly original man. But his greatness as a teacher is not attributed to the fact that he had a coherent system of thought with reference to the technical subjects which were his subject matter while teaching at this College. His greatness, in my submission, transcended mere contributions of doctrine, let alone dogma. It transcended the mere deposit of additional knowledge to the coral reef of knowledge that is ultimately the basis for understanding and wisdom.

He was a great teacher in the sense that Socrates defined a teacher: "the mid-wife of the mind." Or if I may change my figures of speech, he ignited minds that were theretofore inert. He woke us up, all of us. For all of us were students of Morris Cohen, whether we had the great fortune to sit at his feet inside or outside the class room, and had the good fortune to have had from him the illumination, the instigation, and the incitement that the mind requires for its torpid and dormant capacities to come to life. He was a great teacher because nobody could come within range of his personal influence without coming out of it a different man. How different? A new sense of curiosity, a new sense of eagerness about existence, a new sense of the zest of life, a new sense of purpose, and all with a new sense of humility.

Mr. Justice Holmes said there was something of saintliness about Morris Cohen. Now what was there in Professor Cohen, the ruthless, robust, uncompromising pursuer of truth, that deserved the characterization of saintliness? I should say that it was his honesty. I remember hearing Professor Alfred North Whitehead say to a group of teachers—after he had enumerated sixteen or seventeen qualities a good teacher ought to have—that a teacher should be honest, and that is not easy. By honesty one doesn't mean vulgar or ordinary nonlying; it means more than what is called truth-telling. It means searching your insides to know that what you are saying really can stand the test of cross-examination by somebody who knows even more than you do. It means being sure you don't adulterate your remarks with coloration of emotion, of feeling, or of bias. It means that you are not satisfied with clichés and slogans.

How many people who reject ideas know what they are rejecting, and why they are rejecting them? How many people who accept a concept have tested the basis for their acceptance? From one point of view it used to be charged against Morris Cohen that he was destructive—that he was negative. Well, he was negative, in the sense that Socrates was destructive and negative. When a student once complained to Morris Cohen that he was nothing but negative and destructive, he would ask whether Hercules was being destructive and negative when he cleaned out the

Augean stables. After all, the stables were clean, weren't they? And the first duty of man is to make his brain, his mind, his thoughts, his convictions, the things that he professes, clean in the sense of resting on a basis of reflective thought and critical self-cross-examination. I say that Morris Cohen was one of the great instigating, inspiring, radiating teachers of our lifetime. He was that rare thing, a person so critical of self, so determined that nothing should cross his lips for which he isn't ready to accept responsibility, that he made the same exacting demands of his students. And the exactions made those students different people, with an awareness that they must examine their calling, must examine the meaning of their profession whether it was the law (and he influenced an enormous number of men in my profession, whether as practicing lawyers, as law professors, or as judges) or some other calling. He had that magical ability to make life richer and deeper because he had that divine gift of making his students more important than they ever thought themselves to be.

This brings me quite naturally to the fourth devotion to which I am happy to be allowed to bear testimony, namely a library. No name could be more appropriate for a library, and especially the library of The City College, than Morris Cohen's. I won't go as far as Carlyle did when he said "a true university is a library of books," though I have known men to whom that was the only university. But I do say, not wishing in the slightest to diminish the satisfaction we have in our City College buildings and particularly the wonderful new library building, that essentially, a university, an educational institution like this, is *men* and *books*. I am not as austere as Carlyle and so I don't exclude men.

Yet I know of no more fitting way to keep Morris Cohen's memory symbolically alive in the minds of those of us who came directly under his sway and for future generations than through the magnificent new library building. Generation after generation, students here will ask, "Who was Morris Cohen?" "Why is the building named after him?" A library is not a cemetery of dead books. It is an ever-refreshed, ever-enlarged ballet of animated ideas. And so I am rejoiced that it is named in honor of Morris Cohen. For he was a man whom to know was to love. And to have known him either directly or through his life's works, was to have one's life refreshed, enlarged, and fortified.

XVII

Israel's Tenth Anniversary

A dinner in tribute to Israel's historic achievements was held in New York on the occasion of that state's tenth anniversary, May 19, 1958. Mr. Justice Frankfurter's talk followed immediately on the remarks of Dr. Lewis Mumford, who in turn had been preceded by Senator Herbert Lehman, Senator Jacob Javits, Dr. Nahum Goldmann, and Professor Henry Steel Commager. The Justice spoke without a manuscript and his notes consisted solely of the quotations contained herein.

I DO NOT mean to minimize in the slightest the natural anxiety and compassionate concern just expressed, nor do I need to minimize the real danger [that mankind will destroy itself] which led my friend Mumford to make here the speech that he did make. As I listened to him, there was stirred in me a memory of one of the last conversations that I had with Mr. Justice Brandeis, and if I share it with you, my friend Mumford is responsible for it, because the encircling gloom in which he enveloped us deserves a piercing note of faith.

It was in that very anxious, terrible period when the Panzer troops were at the edge, the entrance of what was then called Palestine. I saw Mr. Justice Brandeis when the news was the blackest and he said, "Even if it is all razed to the ground, if the Panzer troops should wipe out all of Palestine, my faith in Palestine, in all that Zionism means is unshaken, because we have proved we can do it."

Now, if it was proved to Louis Brandeis in 1941 that we could do it, what happiness would he have, Senator Lehman, if he were one of us tonight?

And it is on this theme that I should like to say a few words, for the freedom of piercing the future, which is a statesman's duty, is not only not mine yet but is denied to one in my position. Equally can I not enter the area of philosophic history which my friend Commager so convincingly sketched for us. Having been in Israel when it was still Palestine, I do not lack sympathy with the main burden of my friend Goldmann's speech about the special significance of Israel to the Jewish people as a Jewish people.

Mine is a more limited purpose tonight. It is to state in very simple terms the reasons why we are here, whatever other reasons may have brought us here, the reasons that at all events all of us share in being here.

Why are we here? In the first place, to express quiet pride—I hope without self-righteousness—in being the inheritor of a great past and a great past recreated, I say recreated, not restored, in its native soil. We came here to fortify our spirits for the long years of trial that are ahead for mankind, not least for Jews. Finally, we came, you and I, to deepen our understanding of the conditions essential for a free society.

What we are celebrating is neither sectarian nor parochial. It is not restrictive in significance nor local in need. I do not think I use the language of hyperbole if I say that history, democracy, and civilization are vindicated by the beginning of the second decade of Israel.

However tenuous the physical connection between the Jewish people and Israel, it was never severed after the exile. The psychological, or, perhaps still more, the spiritual tie, unique as it is, is, I suppose, as powerful a manifestation as any that history records.

The gathering-in is, too, I should think, a partial relief to the conscience of mankind. With that cold precision of his, Justice Brandeis foresaw this problem even before it came to be in all its ghastly extension. Speaking of the White Paper, which sought to freeze the immigration into Palestine—and I am using the term historically—before Brandeis could have dreamt, before anybody, I should think, could foresee the devilish, systematic endeavor to extirpate and exterminate Jews altogether, even as to that limited attempt to restrict and confine the coming-in of Jews into what is now Israel, he wrote:

> What does the world propose to do with the Jews for whom exile is enforced unless civilization has so reverted to primitivism as to wish the destruction of homeless Jews? It must encourage the proved medium to solve in great measure the problem of Jewish homelessness.

That is as he saw it in May 1939.

So I say that the conscience of the world must be partly, at least, relieved at the ingathering that has taken place in Israel.

Secondly, speaking of the necessary conditions for any free society, Israel certainly is, beyond dispute, a shining manifestation of a free, true democracy; a determined member of the free world. Now, we almost take these achievements for granted, but I think great achievements must be dwelt on, must be intensively considered, their significance regarded, so that we may extract whatever we can extract from history. These are extraordinary achievements. Let me take them one by one. The fructification of the despoiled land. It is such a commonplace. Paeans of praise are so spent upon it that I think there is hardly a realization, even on the part of those who see what has been done, of what had to be undone.

Let me give you a graphic picture of what Palestine was less than one hundred years ago.

In one of his eloquent, nonironically humorous pieces of writing, Mark Twain gave a picture of his visit to Palestine.

I will read it, though it is a bit lengthy, because for me it illustrates, it demonstrates, it makes vivid what has been accomplished, better than anything I have read or any talk I have heard.

Listen to Mark Twain when he came back from there in 1869.

> Palestine sits in sackcloth and ashes. Over it broods the spell of a curse that has withered its fields and fettered its energies. Where Sodom and Gomorrah reared their domes and towers, that solemn sea now floods the plain, in whose bitter waters no living thing exists—over whose waveless surface the blistering air hangs motionless and dead—about whose borders nothing grows but weeds, and scattering tufts of cane, and that treacherous fruit that promises refreshment to parching lips, but turns to ashes at the touch. Nazareth is forlorn; about that ford of Jordan where the hosts of Israel entered the Promised Land with songs of rejoicing, one finds only a squalid camp of fantastic Bedouins of the desert; Jericho the accursed lies a mouldering ruin, to-day, even as Joshua's miracle left it more than three thousand years ago; Bethlehem and Bethany, in their poverty and their humiliation, have nothing about them now to remind one that they once knew the high honor of the Saviour's presence; the hallowed spot where the shepherds watched their flocks by night, and where the angels sang Peace on earth, good will to men, is untenanted by any living creature, and unblessed by any feature that is pleasant to the eye. Renowned Jerusalem itself, the stateliest name in history, has lost all its ancient grandeur, and is become a pauper village; the riches of Solomon are no longer there to compel the

admiration of visiting Oriental queens; the wonderful temple which was the pride and glory of Israel, is gone, and the Ottoman crescent is lifted above the spot where, on that most memorable day in the annals of the world, they reared the Holy Cross. The noted Sea of Galilee, where Roman fleets once rode at anchor and the disciples of the Saviour sailed in their ships, was long ago deserted by the devotees of war and commerce, and its borders are a silent wilderness; Capernaum is a shapeless ruin; Magdala is the home of beggared Arabs; Bethsaida and Chorazin have vanished from the earth, and the "desert places" round about them where thousands of men once listened to the Saviour's voice and ate the miraculous bread, sleep in the hush of a solitude that is inhabited only by birds of prey and skulking foxes.

Palestine is desolate and unlovely. . . . Palestine is no more of this work-day world. It is sacred to poetry and tradition—it is dream-land.[1]

Well, now, 1869 is not so long ago. I almost remember it, but not quite.

Thirdly, the achievement of democracy. We take it for granted. When you think of the conditions under which democracy was established and under which it flourishes in Israel, external difficulties and inherent internal difficulties, I think that the achievement of democracy as a progressive exercise of free men, each a part of the sovereignty of the state, is one of the rarest, one of the most admirable and inspiring manifestations of political skill, of civic devotion, of institutional enterprise.

How did these, to me, extraordinary achievements, come to be?

Several times tonight the word "miracle" was used. And one inevitably speaks of what has been done in Israel as miraculous, as a miracle. Miraculous? Yes; but yet not superhuman. A miracle in the sense in which Herzl foresaw

[1] *The Innocents Abroad* (Hartford, Conn., 1870), pp. 607–608.

the miracle was to be accomplished—by hard, unremitting work. The same thought was expressed by Mr. Justice Holmes when he said that the mode by which the inevitable comes to pass is effort. But effort is not enough, and will is not enough, though without it nothing else matters.

Effort and will must be wisely directed, and that is another great lesson we can all learn from Israel. Israel represents science harnessed to social vision pursued with pertinacity. And it is a happy coincidence, if coincidence it be, something we cannot account for, that the first President of Israel, Chaim Weizmann, should have combined in himself those two indispensable qualifications for high statesmanship, for high achievement, for great civilization, namely, that he was a man of vision who harnessed his science to the achievement of his vision.

You will recall that the most contested feature of the whole business in those early days was summed up in the phrase "absorptive capacity": how many people can live and survive in Israel. And the experts, these limited experts who see acutely the limited things that they do see—it is very important, but you have to see some other things besides—they had figured out almost to a decimal nicety how many people could have a viable existence in Israel. And when Lord Peel asked Dr. Weizmann, "What are you doing at your Institute?" his reply was, "I am creating absorptive capacity."

"I am creating absorptive capacity!" How was he creating it? We are still debating whether basic science is necessary for the well-being of a society. That problem was settled at Rehovath, at the Institute. It was almost settled when the University was founded. The clash of arms had not yet been stilled. The fighting was not over. Compared with today, the population of Israel was what, Dr. Goldmann?—500,000—600,000?

But what was done? The Hebrew University was laid. Because those extraordinary men—as Professor Commager said, that group of men comparable to that extraordinary galaxy of people, the colonists, who came to the United States—because they saw that a democratic society demands knowledge, free inquiry, independent and intrepid search into what was still unknown, basic science was undertaken, while we in the United States are still debating it.

How about the democratic aspect—how did that come to be? Did they decide they were going to be a democracy? Have a constitution? As a matter of fact, they haven't got a written constitution. And, incidentally, they can still survive, can't they, without a written constitution? Indeed, I am not sure that in their circumstances, with their problems, they are not wise in not having one as yet, for reasons that are irrelevant to this occasion.

You cannot have a democracy unless the man, the individual citizen, becomes more than himself in isolation and is forced through public opinion to active participation beyond that cultivated in any other form of organized society. And so I venture to believe in no country—I do not even exclude the United Kingdom—in no country is there such active participation, such a pervasive sense of duty on the part of every citizen, such a collective effort without collectivization, the individual drawing strength from the mass, but not being absorbed by it, as is the case in Israel.

The past is prologue.

I am very glad, indeed, that Dr. Goldmann did not sit down before he indicated the vast problems that are ahead. Perhaps he will forgive me if I put the first of them, the Arab-Jewish problem, in different terms, and speak of it in the larger context of the adjustment of the impact of

Western civilization and Western technology upon the newly awakened peoples in Africa and in Asia. It amounts to the same thing, but certainly that, in my view, has been the most explosive single factor in the whole situation.

The second is the internal cultural situation. Because the ingathering was not merely a question of giving exiles refuge but giving them, as he so eloquently put it, a home.

And even in this agreeable company, one ought not to leave out the very serious economic problems that confront a society which cannot be fully self-reliant, unless it is very largely self-sustaining.

There are those problems ahead. What is the relevance of them to this goodly company? What are you and I going to do about it? What report will we make when on May 19, 1968—for Senator Lehman and I hope to be present then to celebrate with you the beginning of the third decade of Israel—what will we bring as our report of our contribution in this country toward Israel's further fulfillment?

In the first place, it is important to rid ourselves of that American failing of being interested in subjects without knowing about them. I think it is profoundly important, not merely to have this exalted feeling of achievement with which we identify ourselves, but to know with particularity what is going on in Israel, because out of knowledge comes deeper interest, and out of deeper interest comes some form of activity peculiar and congenial to the particular person affected.

Such knowledge must be communicated to others, so that the kind of program that Senator Javits outlines—an area into which I am not free to enter, but I am free to listen—may have the necessary support of public understanding and opinion and desire, to which statesmen, a little late sometimes, but eventually not too late, respond.

Finally, each in his or her different way may make his contribution toward something, toward an enterprise, toward the achievement which I have so sketchily indicated as belonging to us, not merely as Jews, but which belongs to us as part of a world that seeks to forge ahead despite all the retardation, all the limitations, all the setbacks, all the disappointments.

Ultimately, what is the meaning of Israel? May I say, for myself, that what it means is that during the long checkered history of man, Jews have not been the least who have contributed toward a worthy civilization, and in view of the contributions Jews have made in their scattered, non-communal, nonrooted way, one has every right to hope, Jewish contributions will be more effectively, more fruitfully, more continuously, more worthily manifested in that magic atmosphere of Israel, and that what she will do in the future will lead the other nations of the world to call her blessed.

XVIII

Federalism and the Role of the Supreme Court

On September 16, 1958, there gathered in the courtroom of the Supreme Court the heads of the British Commonwealth universities and their hosts, the president and members of the Association of American Universities, who were meeting in Washington. Mr. Justice Frankfurter was called upon to speak to them of matters relevant to their visit. As usual, the remarks were extemporaneous except for a quotation or two around which his talk was constructed in the presence of the audience.

I AM very glad to see President de Kiewiet in the Chief Justice's chair. But I am bound to say I am more regretful that the Chief Justice doesn't sit in it; and so it has fallen to me to exercise the function of honor in greeting you. Now I have sat in this chair for almost twenty years, and I ought to feel at ease in this room. But I don't, in facing you. These are not idle words of flattery. I am awed not by your achievements but by your responsibilities. I thought I ought to know more than the casual gleanings of knowledge that one derives who was for twenty-five years himself a university teacher and had students from parts of the world from which some of you come. And I also, as I told the Vice Chancellor of Bristol University, had some sense of what was going on in what used to be called snobbishly the provincial universities in England, derived from Lord Haldane's *Autobiography*. But, knowing how meager and fragile such casual knowledge is—is bound to be—I thought I would inform myself a little bit as to the range and diversity of the universities in the English-speaking world. And so I thought I would take a few minutes to look through the *Commonwealth Universities Annual for 1958*. What a monstrous, mastodonic volume that is! Thirteen hundred pages. But I can assure you that when I began the minutes extended into hours, and I found myself paging that whole volume, resting here and there some little time in getting a sense of what has been going on with such rapidity in the university world within the English-speaking world. I was struck with the variety, the range, the differences in environment, the complexities of the problems that confront universities, whether they are old—the oldest, Oxford—or young. I believe Dr. Adams' Rhodesia is the youngest—am I right about that? Anyhow, 1957 is pretty recent.

When I say I am awed by your presence I do not mean to say by your personal presence, because I have had a few mitigating familiarities among you. But when I contemplate the relation between modern society and education, then I am bound to say I am awed by all that you represent. I suppose you will agree if I say that the vital nature of politics in a democratic society is as a process of education. But the converse is equally true. The process of education enormously influences the spirit and direction of politics. You have all heard—but it bears repeating, because from my point of view it is so far-reaching—the reply of Einstein when he was asked by an anxious inquirer, "Why is it, when we have made such enormous strides, such vast progress, in the so-called conquest of nature, in the penetration of things heretofore unknown and mysterious, why is it when we have made such enormous progress in the field of science that we have done so badly, on the whole, in grappling with international problems?" And then that wonderfully childlike genius that Einstein was, indulged in, or rather instinctively gave, one of his seraphic smiles and said, "The answer is very simple: physics is so much more simple than politics."

I am sorry that you are here when the Court isn't sitting and arguments aren't heard on issues that even today are elsewhere often the contest of arms rather than the contest of reason. You are here in the institution which has the rather unique function of umpiring the internal problems of our country. I still suggest to you that the best book that's ever been written about America was written in 1835 by that extraordinarily penetrating young man, Alexis de Tocqueville. And not the least of his prescient insights was that he saw very early that almost any question of state that arises in this country—in view of the nature of our kind of government—must eventually come here, to the bar of this Court, at that lectern, where counsel present their conflicting claims, with at least two sides to a controversy. It is entirely easy to settle any question if only one principle is involved. But the hang of it is that most questions, all questions that are difficult, have a conflict of at least two so-called principles. At the bar of this Court many a controversy that elsewhere is still settled by the conquest of arms is, eventually anyhow, settled by force of reason. And Tocqueville saw that very early. And why is that so, and why is it uniquely true of this country, in the room in which you are sitting, in which these contests of reason, of argument, of respective claims rationally put forward, occur?

In the first place—and here I am addressing myself more particularly to my friends of the British Isles and some of the other places, but not to my friends from Australia and Canada and India—in the first place, ours is a federalism, which means, of course, that the powers of government are diffused between two sets of governments, except for the city in which you happily are, at least for a few hours. Except for the District of Columbia, the City of Washington, there is not a foot of ground in this vast country which does not represent an interplay of political authority in which two governments are simultaneously operating, the state government and the federal government. And a distribution of what belongs to which, no matter what genius of constitution-making may have delineated it—such are the limitations of the human mind, of the human imagination—necessarily begets difficult problems of construction, problems calling for resolution. And it is in this building, in this room, where the arguments take place, and in the little room across the hall where the conferences of the Court take place, that those determinations are made.

No doubt all of you know that. Every Englishman knows that. But between knowing a fact and feeling it, between being able to speak it in words and comprehending it in its entirety, there lies, it has been my experience, a vast gulf. The differences between a federal system of government like ours, with powers expressed in a written document necessarily calling for construction by somebody —and the somebody is this Court—and a unitary system where no such problems arise, are very great indeed.

I will allow myself to read to you a statement of the problem by a most esteemed judge, from my point of view a judge second to none in the English-speaking world, the present Chief Justice of Australia. As you know, as the Australians know, and the Canadians know, and the Indians know, and the British know in a casual way, appeals from Australian judgments sometimes go up to the Judicial Committee of the Privy Council. Chief Justice Owen Dixon and some of his predecessors must have been irked by what they felt was the incomprehension of even eminent English judges regarding the nature of a federal system. And so let me read you what Sir Owen Dixon wrote only the other day—a few months ago—and see if you don't agree that while his thought may be nasty, his expression is charming.

"Federalism," he wrote, "is a form of government the nature of which is seldom adequately understood in all its bearing by those whose fortune it is to live under a unitary system. The problems of federalism and the considerations governing their solution assume a different aspect to those whose lives are spent under the operation of a federal constitution, particularly if by education, practice, and study they have been brought to think about the constitutional conceptions and modes of reasoning which belong to federalism as commonplace and familiar ideas. A unitary system presents no analogies and indeed, on the contrary, it forms a background against which many of the conceptions and distinctions inherent in federalism must strike the mind as strange and exotic refinements." If you find it difficult to understand our ways, I suggest you recall Sir Owen's remarks, that is, those of you who do not live under a federal system.

But ours is a unique scheme of government even as compared with other federalisms: Canada, Australia, and India. In each of these three countries there is a written constitution. In each of these three countries there is a parceling out of that which is concentrated in England and in France and in Belgium, in Scotland. (The people of Scotland won't mind if I take them as a separate nation.) There is an extra aspect to our scheme of things, which makes this Court exercise responsibility not exercised by the Supreme Court of Canada, the Supreme Court of India, or the High Court of Australia. It is this. The Constitution of the United States is the oldest—to some people that's a fault—in the Western world. The men who framed it were, to an extraordinary degree, a constellation of very able men. But they were not godlike, they were limited by human vision, limited by their own imagination, and by their own experience. But they were very wise men so they did not try to formulate a Constitution designed for the undefined and illimitable future, as they conceived the destiny of this country to be, with particularity. They wrote in broad outlines so that the future would not be foreclosed, so that the past would not too much govern the future. And thus it is, and I think largely for that reason, that so far as the *structure* of our government is concerned, as formulated by fifty-odd men in Philadelphia in 1787, the *structure* has remained unchanged. There have been amendments to the constitution, but no *structural* amendments. In amendments relating to the right of women to vote, election of Senators by the people directly and not by the subordinate legislatures of the states, and a few other amendments, no drastic changes in the distribution of political power within our federalism were made.

Not until after and as the result of the Civil War was there a change in the distribution of governmental power, the change that was then made by the amendments, the so-called War Amendments. And those amendments are the source of the greatest difficulties and the most challenging problems to come before this Court. The amendments were framed in inevitably vague terms, considering the purposes they had in mind. They put limitations upon state powers which theretofore had not existed. Those are the famous clauses of which you must have read at least scraps in the newspapers, those are the amendments which prohibit any state from depriving any person of life, liberty, or property without due process of law or deny to any person the equal protection of the laws. And therefore, every enactment of every state, every action by the governor of a state, any governmental act of any of the forty-eight, soon to be forty-nine, states, may be challenged at the bar of this Court on the ground that such action, such legislation, is a deprivation of liberty without due process of law or denies the equal protection of the laws.

Now those phrases, those crucial phrases "due process of law" and "equal protection of the laws"—what is "due," what is "equal," in a world in which there cannot always be uniformities—those are the phrases of the Constitution, saying no more than I have quoted, that beget the difficulties that come to the bar of this Court and that very anxiously challenge the thoughts not only of the judges but of the people of this country.

Let me illustrate very concretely the difference in having such a restriction upon the action of state governments in our Constitution as against the absence of such a provision in the federal constitutions of Canada, Australia, and India. There is no such provision in the Indian Constitution, which was the product of careful study by that very distinguished jurist of India, Sir Benegal Rau, who spent several years here studying how our scheme of things works, and then recommended against inclusion of such a restriction upon the states of India. My mind recalls, as I speak, that preceding the first World War, a Liberal Government under Asquith, in proposing the Home Rule Bill —which died, of course, when World War I broke out— rejected an amendment to the Home Rule Bill designed for Ireland which would have put into that measure a due-process clause like ours. And that debate is well worth reading by any student of the subject because many of the leading lawyers in England, then in Parliament, took part in the debate. Some of the best of them studied our experience and said those are too indefinite instruments of language with which to entrust courts for judicial judgment.

By great good fortune I am able to illustrate the point even more vividly by an item in this morning's paper. Prime Minister Diefenbaker of Canada introduced a measure in Ottawa yesterday, a measure that would put into law, in substance, the American Bill of Rights—due process of law, equal protection, and all the rest of it—with *two* vital differences. In the first place, Prime Minister Diefenbaker said, "I am introducing this as a *statute*, not as an amendment to our Constitution"—a statute capable of change by Parliament the next day, if it so chooses. And secondly, his bill would impose such a "bill of rights" not as restrictions upon provincial powers, but merely restrictions upon dominion powers. But our Constitution enables this Court to strike down acts of Congress and acts of every one of the forty-eight States and action by the President of the United States, the justification for such decisions being nothing else than the phrase "due process of law" or "equal protection of the laws." Of course, the Court isn't a class in English composition and the Constitution isn't merely a literary document. It is a scheme of government with a great deal of history behind it, with antecedents of thought, of purpose, and so forth. Nevertheless, the ultimate justification for nullifying or saying that what Congress did, what the President did, what the legislature of Massachusetts or New York or any other state did was beyond its power, is that provision of the Constitution which protects liberty against infringement without due process of law. There are times, I can assure you—more times than once or twice—when I sit in this chair and wonder whether that isn't too great a power to give to any nine men, no matter how wise, how well disciplined, how disinterested. It covers the whole gamut of political, social, and economic activities.

I thought the best way—as illuminating as any—to bring home to you what constitutes the function of this third branch of our government, which has the ultimate determination of constitutional or unconstitutional action by the other two branches, is to read something remote from present controversies that was written by a very great man—in my judgment the greatest intellect who ever sat on this Court.

This is what Justice Holmes said more than fifty years ago. And please bear in mind that this was said by a man who had been the Chief Justice of the then most distinguished state court in the land, the Massachusetts Supreme Judicial Court. He sat for twenty years as a judge up there, with vast experience and, I suppose, probably with the most copious learning of any judge we have ever had. This is what he wrote to his friend Sir Frederick Pollock.

> Yes,—here I am—and more absorbed, interested and impressed than ever I dreamed I might be. The work of the past is a finished book—locked up far away, and a new and solemn volume opens. The variety and novelty to me of the questions, the remote spaces from which they come, the amount of work they require, all help the effect. I have written on the constitutionality of part of the Constitution of California, on the power of the Railroad Commissioner of Arkansas, on the question whether a law of Wisconsin impairs the obligation of the plaintiff's contract. I have to consider a question between a grant of the U.S. in aid of a military road and an Indian reservation on the Pacific coast. I have heard conflicting mining claims in Arizona and whether a granite quarry is "Minerals" within an exception in Railway grant, and fifty other things as remote from each other as these.[1]

[1] Mark DeWolfe Howe, ed., *The Holmes-Pollock Letters: The Correspondence of Mr. Justice Holmes and Sir Frederick Pollock, 1874–1935*, 2 vols. (Cambridge, Mass., 1941), I, 109–110.

Well, since then the complexity and range of issues before the Court have increased. The population of the country has nearly doubled. It is a great pity that you aren't traveling through this country in a slow thirty-five miles-per-hour car, in order to get a sense within yourself, not merely knowing it abstractly, a sense within yourself of the varieties of climate, of resources, of preoccupations among the people of the United States, all of which vast interests and claims and habits and mores and whatnot which have to be dealt with by the lawyers who talk, sometimes well and sometimes not so well, at the Bar of this Court and finally have to be accommodated by the Court. At all events, with us they can't talk forever as they are allowed to in the English courts; the volume of business precludes it. Parenthetically, it is our experience that the less time you give these lawyers, the more they say.

I think you will soon have to depart for pleasanter quarters [the White House], but let an old colleague of yours, if you will so let me still describe myself, say this from the fullness of my heart and from the depth of my conviction: When I read as I read in this *Annual* that there are 40,000 British Commonwealth University teachers, when I reflect what it means that some eighty to ninety universities are represented in this room, scattered over something like seventeen countries, when I consider the demands upon adjustment to environments as different as those that you represent, and then ponder over the fact that whether the universities are in this country or in Rhodesia or in India or in New Zealand or in Eire or Northern Ireland, nevertheless all going back to certain deep roots from which all of us spring, I am at once awed and inspired. Certain hopes, certain anxieties, certain beliefs about human nature and the extent to which a democratic society best and most fruitfully fulfills those desires naturally are stirred in one.

One of our greatest Presidents, Thomas Jefferson, left instructions for the epitaph on his tombstone. And I refer to that again and again and again in my own feeling and thinking about life because it so powerfully demonstrates what is important, what is significant, ultimately significant, and what is not. Here was Thomas Jefferson, who was the governor of his state, who was Ambassador to France, the first Secretary of State of the United States, Vice President, and a two-term President, and what did he ask to have written on his tombstone? Not one of those things, not one. "Here was buried Thomas Jefferson, author of the Declaration of American Independence, of the Statute of Virginia for Religious Freedom and Father of the University of Virginia." When you come to think of it, why wasn't he right? Aren't the forces, the ideas, the desires, the visions represented by those three accomplishments the things that are determinative of all else? And so I feel that in this troubled and anguished world, when I think of you representing these 40,000 university teachers, the institutions which nourished them and the students whose lives they help unfold, when I think of the burdens that are yours, when I think of the rewards and satisfactions in life that are also yours in carrying those burdens, then you will let me say as my last words, "Godspeed, as you go forward in your endeavors."

«XIX»

Learned Hand's Fiftieth Anniversary as a Federal Judge

Judge Learned Hand's fiftieth anniversary as a federal judge was celebrated at a ceremony in the Federal Court House at Foley Square on April 10, 1959. Mr. Justice Frankfurter's remarks on this felicitous occasion were recorded as follows:

LEST POOR Learned Hand suffocate, one of us ought to desist from adding to the outpour of libations. Age and the precious friendship of half a century may perhaps appropriately put the uncongenial task upon me of rescuing the man from the legend. Incredible as it may sound, L. Hand has, if not defects, at least limitations. I have time to deal with only one of them, but an important one. He has not met the most important teaching of Socrates: "Know thyself." As an autobiographer, he is wholly unreliable. With ample opportunities for self-knowledge and after he had reached the Psalmist's age, this is the way he summed up his life: "Uneventful, unadventurous, easy, safe and pleasant." I ask you, can you imagine a characterization of Learned Hand conveyed by five more inapt and inaccurate adjectives than those five? His life "uneventful"?—uneventful, if events occur only in the world of action and not in the arena of the mind. "Unadventurous?"—unadventurous only if adventure requires the scaling of Mount Everest and the crossing of Antarctica, only if there be no adventures of thought. "Easy"?—has it been easy all these years to find clear meaning in the obscurities and mumbo-jumbo of the nine Delphic Oracles, at pain of a spanking for not finding clarity in darkness? "Safe"?—has life been safe, has it been secure, for one who has been buffeted and battered by his own doubts beyond almost anybody? "Pleasant"? Well, perhaps he's got something there. But it's a sly bit of truth. For his life would not have had so much pleasure if *he* hadn't been there.

What a sorry showing in the use of language for one who by common consent has been the best wielder of English speech on the bench since the pen of Holmes came to rest.

Let me teach him to be truthful even about himself! Instead of his five wholly misleading adjectives, I offer you these five: daring, romantic, antediluvian, sophisticated, lucky. "Daring," because in a world with increasing pressures toward conformity he has gaily and solemnly dared to be himself; "daring," because he has challenged intolerance and prejudice even when supported by patriotic fervor and the voice of the multitude. "Romantic," because the windows of his mind have been open to all the winds of doctrine, giving hostages to no established truth and ready to find the Holy Grail in the least likely places. "Antediluvian"? Surely a judge is that who seeks to be guided by the reason of which he is a trustee and delegate and not an inventor, a judge who has a humble conception of his office and does not deem himself empowered to rebuild the world according to his heart's desire. "Sophisticated" in that he does not confound the familiar with the necessary, questions his own basic premises even while acting upon them until he gets better ones.

Finally, how lucky he has been. "Lucky" in having attained that which makes all the rest of life bearable—a happy marriage, sheer luck. And "lucky" in his failures.

He was lucky when, having offered himself to the people of the State of New York, they rejected him for a seat on the Court of Appeals. Surely his personal life is much happier in New York than it would have been in Albany, and with every respect for the importance of the great court in Albany and the eminent men who have graced it, the range of problems with which he has been concerned on the federal bench are in the mass more teasing and exciting than those that would have occupied his mind in Albany. And how lucky he was that he did not win in that odd lottery by which men get picked for the Supreme Court of the United States. For one thing, down there his views would have been diluted by eight-ninths instead of by merely two-thirds. Again, the controversies at Washington are almost inevitably more strident than the quietude of Foley Square. And with all the plenitude of gifts, I don't think L. Hand is possessed of the *gaudium certaminis*, the joy of battle. Moreover, his freedom of utterance would have been much more circumscribed, he would have felt much more restricted within the curtilage of the Court and we would have been denied all these years the moral influence and stimulus of his eloquent and courageous free spirit.

His writings are a heartening proof that the achievements of excellence and the fertilization of thought are not dependent upon place. Although Holmes felt that the rightful place for Hand, while still a District Judge, was on the Supreme Bench and although for half my life I left no opportunity unavailed of to promote that end, I still think he is lucky. But we are even luckier that he has put his gifts to the uses to which he has put them. Long after all of us in this room are gone, he will continue to serve society so long as law exercises its indispensable role in helping to unravel the tangled skein of the human situation.

XX

Calvert Magruder

In 1959, when Calvert Magruder retired as chief judge of the Court of Appeals for the First Circuit, after twenty years service on that bench, Mr. Justice Frankfurter wrote the dedication to Judge Magruder for the *Harvard Law School Yearbook* and another piece of appreciation for the *Harvard Law Review* 72:1201 (June 1959). Although there is some overlap in the two pieces, both are reproduced below without the editorial mayhem that would be necessary to avoid the repetition.

In giving public utterance to anything even truthfully appreciative of Calvert Magruder, one finds himself inhibited by a cramping awareness of the Judge's modesty. Even his modesty is not so powerful as to be contagious, but at least it is compelling enough to make one careful not to offend it. While it may surprise him to be told so, he will have to yield to the fact that among the hundreds of teachers in the long history of the Harvard Law School he occupies a unique position. We have had, particularly in the early days, sitting judges who did some teaching; we have had former judges who became teachers; we have had teachers who became judges. Magruder alone went from the chair to the bench and continued as a teacher, to the great benefit of the bench and the school.

I cannot speak of him as a student; he shunned all my courses. I can, however, speak of myself as his pupil, albeit a derivative pupil. I have the good fortune to have had over the years seven law clerks who came to me after their postgraduate judicial year with Judge Magruder. Different as these seven men were in their virtues and in their limitations, as men of high quality always are different, they had certain professional and human qualities in common. As the phenomena of these common qualities repeated themselves, their common source of inspiration and influence—Calvert Magruder—became manifest.

At this point, my awareness of Magruder's modesty asserts itself. I must not attribute to him innate qualities of these admirable law clerks, not attribute to him the enveloping atmosphere of the Harvard Law School, which these young men more unconsciously than consciously doubtlessly absorbed. But making even the most generous allowances for the shaping influences that were unrelated to Calvert Magruder, it cannot be doubted that what he meant to these men and therefore what he did to them cropped out too frequently and too prominently during their year with me to be denied. Indeed, as occasion from time to time arose, I had to struggle not a little to maintain my independence against the strong feeling of my Magruder law clerks that in my attitude toward some judicial problem I was not walking the straight and narrow and sensible and relaxed path of Magruder. The criteria of relevance and candor and earthiness by which I was judged were the Magruder criteria. In a word, he was for them *the* image of a judge. And this was so, not merely as to substance but as to form. For in their year with Judge Magruder they were made to realize, as all who read his opinions are made to realize, that form and substance in legal opinions are not opposite or alien ingredients but constitute a fused whole. The judicial office does not automatically generate a style as limpid as Magruder's, but we can all try to do better than we do, and I should like to think that the Magruder standard set for me by his former law clerks was not wholly unheeded.

I have said that in Magruder substance and form are not disjointed. Still less is there a separation in him between the judge and the man. As good fortune brought me a succession of these Magruder law clerks, I became even more conscious than I had been made through my own relations with him that, while he had exceptional endowments as a lawyer which were reflected in him as a judge, this professional side of him was infused by his qualities as a man.

I have emphasized modesty as the dominant characteristic of him. But in him modesty is not an expression of shyness or self-depreciation or self-distrust. It has, I believe, deeper sources and deeper consequences than shyness often has in men. I am not sure that he knows this. Part of Magruder's hardheadedness is lack of undue introspection. He is not merely modest about himself in the sense that he doesn't think too much of himself. He is modest about man—and even man become judge. I am sure that had Mr. Justice Holmes known of Calvert Magruder's judicial career he would have found in him a true disciple of his deepest convictions that the first duty of a judge is to remember that he is not God. By no means does this imply that he has shrunk from a judge's duty to reach results not to his own personal liking, any more than his modesty restrained his critical judgment from differing with the mighty. The quality of Mr. Justice Brandeis' work was not often open to criticism, particularly by a lad fresh from the Law School, and there was an awesome aspect about him that did not readily loosen tongues. Yet it was Magruder of whom he said, "He was the best critic I ever had." It is, I believe, these human qualities of

Magruder that made him so: his sense of relevance, his respect for the intrinsic unawed by position, the simplicity of his nature, and, not least, his acute sense of craftsmanship.

If from the inadequate things that I have said there does not emerge my affection for the man, admiration for the judge, it would prove that I am wholly devoid of the art of innuendo. If I expressed in direct language my feelings for the man and my respect for the judge I would offend his modesty, so I will stop.

From time to time Calvert Magruder has reminded me with innocent malice, the only kind of which he is capable, that he took none of my three courses. He could not thus hide from me his light under a bushel. On a hunch, limited as my awareness of his qualities then was, I selected him as the first law clerk to Mr. Justice Brandeis. It was a good guess—the art of life, we are told, is accurate guessing on inadequate data—for the Justice said of him: "Among all my law clerks Magruder was the best critic I had." The reaches of this encomium, considering the gifted men who were Magruder's successors! It not only implied his intellectual acumen; for Mr. Justice Brandeis did not leave much scope for the critic. It also conveyed Magruder's charming faculty of easy human relations. The overwhelming personality of the Justice intimidated most people and made them self-consciously reticent.

Over the years Magruder has amassed vast experience in the diversified legal fields he has tilled and through the versatile roles he has played in the law—law teacher, government lawyer and administrator, judge. Wherever he found himself he performed with distinction. These professional opportunities and responsibilities have made for depth and breadth. But he has, to an extent rare in men, happily retained the pith and savor of what he was as a lad. What so delighted the austere Mr. Justice Brandeis in the young Magruder was his spontaneous recognition that in the realm of the mind there is no hierarchical deference.

To trace men's qualities to their roots is usually an illusory enterprise. Yet I am tempted to believe that Magruder's uninhibited way of dealing with intellectual issues derives from his strong sense of relevance and, paradoxical as it may sound, his modesty. If reasoning does not hold water, what difference does it make who employs it? If writing is infelicitous, such it appears, no matter who the author, to the critical eye of Magruder, himself a telling and engaging writer. While Magruder's modesty leads to self-depreciation, it does not generate intellectual confusion. It makes him as exacting of others as of himself in dealing with intellectual issues. While no one could have a higher regard for the office of judge, he does not confuse the occupant with the office. The clarity of his mind and the modesty of his character make him dominantly aware of humility as perhaps the prime judicial requisite, the quality of rigorous self-criticism and of not confounding a desired result with the judicial process, formulated in Mr. Justice Holmes' well-known remark, "The first duty of a judge is to remember that he is not God."

This is very far from implying that Magruder represents the slot-machine theory of adjudication which holds that one can find an answer for every legal problem in the law reports, or even in the best of legal writings, or by means of merely syllogistic reasoning. Cardozo's admirable discussion of the creative aspect of a judge's work did not come to Magruder as revelation. He has not been afraid to pioneer within the limits allowable to a judge for pioneering. He represents that happy blend of judicial caution and valor about which Sir Frederick Pollock has written, and he has achieved it, I believe, because of his happy blend of a sense of relevance and modesty.

Barring the cases which present issues that indisputably call for review by the Supreme Court and that very large number of cases in which review is out of question, the disposition of petitions for certiorari involves competing considerations that cannot be resolved by a fixed calculus. Naturally enough, an important factor in the exercise of the Court's discretionary judgment is the weight of the opinion below, particularly where the problem is new and may fruitfully await the maturing process of further consideration in the lower courts. When petitions for certiorari from decisions in which Judge Magruder wrote have come before the Court, such has been the quality of his opinions, the persuasiveness of his reasoning, and the confinement of decision to its proper scope, that on more than one occasion one has been led to say to his brethren, "Were we to bring the case here, could we improve on Magruder?"

What he says gains weight from the way he says it. The attractiveness of his writing does not only derive from the quality of his style. His opinions irradiate what may fairly be called moral qualities, particularly candor and complete absence of pretense in all its manifestations, from stuffiness to spurious learning. We all love Dr. Johnson for his well-known act of penance at Litchfield, but how many of us imitate his example when occasion offers? Thus, one is delighted to find this opening sentence in an opinion by Judge Magruder: "This case illustrates the perils of misunderstanding incident to the drafting of a judicial opinion," followed by a charming exposition of his own fallibility. (A different example of edifying and illuminating candor is a recent elucidation by him of that normally dreary problem, what constitutes a "final decision" for purposes of appealability under federal jurisdictional acts.) If I were to summarize the quality of Magruder's writing, I would say that he writes as he talks. It is the colloquial talk of a cultivated man. The effect is, as Professor Plucknet describes Maitland's writing, "one of gay intimacy with a lively companion." I must hasten to disavow a seeming comparison of Magruder with Maitland lest I offend his distaste for excessive praise.

The edict of time precluded my having had the good fortune of being one of Magruder's law clerks. Happily, I have been the beneficiary of the inspiring lessons which his law clerks took away from their experience with him. A goodly number of my law clerks came to me after they had been with him whom they invariably called "The Judge." I was subjected to the invigorating discipline of having my labors tested by the touchstone of judicial qualities which those Magruder products so rightly admired in him.

When kind friends gave me a send-off from Cambridge to Washington, I ventured to say, in a moment of self-revelation, that the criterion by which I would care to have my judicial work judged would be the extent to which it reflected the standards appropriate for a member of the Harvard Law School faculty. Judge Magruder superbly meets this test. Happily, he is not retiring from judicial work. He will become a judge-at-large, fertilizing, as it were, the entire federal judicial system and giving to it those conspicuous judicial gifts which for twenty years he has contributed to the First Circuit.

«« XXI »»

Felix S. Cohen

Felix S. Cohen (1907–1953) was the son of Morris Cohen, the Justice's Harvard roommate and longtime friend. Like his father, he was concerned with the philosophy of the law, although he also spent much of the brief time allotted him as a government lawyer and private practitioner. After his premature death, Felix Cohen's wife collected his essays on jurisprudence and published them under the title *Legal Conscience.* The book was published by the Yale University Press in 1960, and his namesake, Mr. Justice Frankfurter, wrote the introduction for it.

BARRING THE rare exception of a seminal paper by the author of transforming thought, an Einstein or a Mendel (and there does not come to mind a comparably influential paper in the sociological domain), for a powerful impact writings seem to require propulsion within the hard covers of a book. His *Handbook of Federal Indian Law* established Felix Cohen as the unrivalled authority within that field. It became the vade mecum of all concerned with its problems, administrators, legislators, lawyers, friends and exploiters of Indians; it was an acknowledged guide for the Supreme Court in Indian litigation. This *Handbook* gave intimations of a scholarship that had cultural dimensions and a philosophic temper. Nor could the discerning reader of his occasional papers in diverse periodicals, some of them less accessible than law reviews, fail to be struck with the freshness and trenchancy of their author's mind. But even those of us who followed the unfolding of Felix Cohen's powers with increasing esteem and admiration must, I am confident, derive an intensified realization of his qualities and their enduring fruit from this collection of his writings.

The episodic character of his essays and their intermittent appearance required that they be gathered into this corpus fully to reveal the breadth and depth of his learning, the originality of his thought and the felicity of its formulation, his enlistment in humane causes, above all the cause of a broadly based civilized community, as reflecting not instinctive, however generous, prejudices, but the report of rational inquiry insofar as reason can give guidance in analyzing and understanding the bias-laden and intractable problems of society.

We now see that his thinking on technical philosophical problems, such as "What is a Question?" his discussion of so-called technical legal questions, his disentanglement of the snarls in which the uninformed find themselves caught when confronted with our Indian problems, the deceptive prejudices which bar clear thinking about the implications of democracy—these major concerns of Felix Cohen were for him not disparate preoccupations nor did they receive unrelated illumination from his mind and pen.

While his thinking was organic, in that he saw interrelations where others dealt with discrete instances, Felix Cohen was not a system-builder. It is significant that more than once he quoted the wise man who said that philosophic systems are true in so far as they affirm and false in so far as they deny. He was a follower of Mr. Justice Holmes' conviction that the most important feature of philosophic systems is their insight and not their logical structure or symmetry. Felix Cohen's devotion was to truth-seeking—to a process never completed—not to any ultimates, either his own or that of others. He was relentless in applying reason, even in areas of human concern where lazier or more dogmatic temperaments denied themselves the liberating influence of reason.

Reading this volume, one cannot forego a feeling of sadness that Felix Cohen was allowed to run not more than half his course. But the more dominant feeling with which one is left by the expansion of one's horizon and the call to honest thinking that we owe to this volume, is gratitude to Felix Cohen for the fullness of a lifetime into which he crowded twenty-five years of thought and deed, and gratitude to his wife for the great gift of this collection.

XXII

The Profession of the Law

On April 30, 1960, the Council of the Harvard Law School Association held its annual meeting in Cambridge. Mr. Justice Frankfurter was the guest of honor on this occasion. In the afternoon of that day he spoke to the students of the Law School and in the evening to the members of the council and the faculty. At the evening ceremony, a bust of the Justice by Miss Eleanor Platt was given to the Law School and accepted by President Pusey. The entire proceedings of the occasion were recorded and published by the Law School. The two talks by the Justice reported below were taken from this pamphlet, *Occasional Pamphlet Number Three: Proceedings in Honor of Mr. Justice Frankfurter and Distinguished Alumni.* The recipients of the awards to the alumni on this occasion were Professor Samuel Williston, then in his ninety-ninth year, Judge Learned Hand, whose bust by Eleanor Platt was already in the possession of the Law School, and Harrison Tweed, of the New York bar.

JUSTICE FRANKFURTER: The old adage that the more things change, the more they remain the same is falsified by this audience. I cannot believe that in the more naïve, or more sophisticated time, I don't know which, of my student days in this Law School, on such a lovely Saturday afternoon, curiosity would have driven so many of us indoors to see what a creature like me, if you will a Justice, looked like, and how he behaved, perchance under provocation.

I don't suppose that Dean Griswold, when he asked me to come here this afternoon—and unlike you I subserviently obey any direction from the Dean—I don't suppose he asked me to come here to present myself as an anthropological exhibit.

We all live by illusions, and why not, so long as they don't hurt other people. And so I like to think that although it was fifty-seven years ago I entered these halls, and in those days we were rather simple and puritan, and content with—what shall I say—the very simple accommodations of Austin Hall, although I think it was only yesterday, nevertheless, it was fifty-seven years ago—I come back to these halls as the great figure of Grecian mythology who had to touch earth every once in a while to regain even his divine strength.

I should like to come here even more frequently than opportunity affords, to touch that detachment and disinterestedness of yours, that desire to understand a problem before reaching a result. I should like to come here more frequently, and I don't think it would do any harm even to the other eight members of the Supreme Court.

Most naturally, I thought not a little about what I should say to the kind of young men I would meet here today, who, I forget, are no longer in the antediluvian age when women were too dangerous to mix with men as students. I naturally ask myself what is it that I should have liked to have heard from a Justice of the Supreme Court in my student days, and particularly one who had touched the law in almost every aspect of legal activity.

I may well have given myself the wrong answer; I can vouch many witnesses to the fact that I often give myself the wrong answer. But I thought that if I had been a student and were asked what should I like to hear from one who has been out in the world of law for fifty-odd years, I should like to have him tell me what expectations I am entitled to entertain that following the law, in any of its manifold manifestations, will bring a fulfilling life. What is there that gives enlargement of view, an expansive outlook to one whose calling is the law?

It is to that theme that I should like to say a few words before I open myself up to the fusillade of questions from this eager and, what shall I say, sanguinary body.

Now, in the first place, you are preparing to enter—and some of you are on the eve of entering—a profession that has behind it a history of some seven or eight centuries of continuous functioning. Well, that is something . . . to be a part of a great march of history. It is a great deal. And particularly is it something when that of which you are a part stretches a millenium, as does the legal profession. It is a profession that is concerned with matters of the mind; the mind, and not the imagination, is the instrument of our activities. I don't mean to be so naïve as to think that the mind is compartmented from the feelings. I don't mean to be so ignorant of what Freud has shown regarding the deep subconscious forces that govern what we think, and our reasons, and conclusions. But it is a fact that the conscious materials of our profession are things of the mind, processes of reasoning.

Now to have behind you eight centuries of history is a very comforting fact. But I am not here to give you comfort. I am not here to flatter you. That is too often the tendency of those who speak to the young in our troubled days: telling them we have made a mess of things, but that you, youth, are going to set this world aright. I don't believe that for one minute. Nor do I hope to offer what the elders do in talking to the young, being smug or pompous, making the assumption that they have great wisdom to bring to the young, which the young should follow.

But I do say that to belong to a profession with such a past as that of the law, though all of it is not entirely glorious or infallible, is an honor. To belong to a profession that has had the great history of the legal profession, a profession that is concerned with the things of the mind, with subjecting questions to the reasoning processes and justification by reason, is a great tradition, in which you will soon become an integral part. I do not mean that you carry around with you a little private museum of which you can be proud. A tradition, if it is worthy of the name, is not wealth hoarded; it is a dynamic energy to be applied. It is a great tradition that the legal profession is entitled to claim for itself in the unfolding of modern constitutional government by law.

Nor does that mean that you must be a part of the government. It does mean that every lawyer belongs to a system which, in the course of seven or eight centuries, has done mightily to bring about as much of civilization as we have today. It may be said that it is not too much that we have achieved, but yet it is a great deal as compared with the alternatives. It is the legal profession beyond any other calling that is concerned with those establishments, those processes, those criteria, those appeals to reason and right, which have had a dominant share in begetting a civilized society.

And that means a learned profession. That means drawing on the juices of your life, as Professor Freund indicated, from almost every domain of learning, because if the law is concerned with the regulation of problems concerning society, then it is necessary to be informed or at least aware of the multitudinous, multifarious forces with which society is concerned, and which affect society.

So that in becoming a lawyer, in whatever capacity—on which I will speak in a minute—you attach yourselves to a great heritage which, to be true to, must be pursued in the context of that heritage. Which means a deep and wide cultural life. No lawyer is entitled to be deemed a lawyer who doesn't keep abreast in his own mind, through reading, through which we gain what the past has afforded, through wide and persistent reading, with what it is that society is concerned with, and about.

Most of you will practice this profession—I assume that is right. Am I right about that, Dean Griswold? Most of these young men and young women will be practicing lawyers.

It is the fashion today, or perhaps the tendency or temptation of today, to think rather ill of being "merely a lawyer." "Merely a lawyer." I do not hold that view. I think a person who throughout his life is nothing but a practicing lawyer fulfills a very great and essential function in the life of society. Think of the responsibilities on the one hand, and the satisfactions on the other, to be a lawyer in the true sense. And what does that mean?

Only Thursday I heard a case—and this is an experience to which I must submit almost every week—I listened to an unfolding of the facts in which a lawyer gave advice to his client that he was entitled to do thus and so, that it was right for him to do what he planned to do. And I said to one of my colleagues, on one side of me, "This is a typical case of unwise advice by a lawyer." He stopped short with the advice that what his client was about to do was within the law—without asking the next question, "Is it wise to insist on your legal right?"

Again and again and again during my twenty-one years or so on the Court, I have been appalled at the lack of wisdom of lawyers in giving advice, on which they might get vindication in the highest court in the land, but the upshot of which would be, and often is, great damage to their clients.

And that is so because lawyers forget what Mr. Justice Brandeis constantly reminded people, that a lawyer is "a counselor at law." It isn't his job merely to say, "I have looked up the precedents, and I know them," or, "I construe this statute to mean thus and so, and you may do thus, or may not do thus." He is a counselor. He is a trustee to the wise conduct of his client. To be sure, if he says to his client, "This is perfectly within the law, it is morally not reprehensible, but it is unwise for these reasons for you to persist in this legal right of yours," and client then says, "Well, that is for me to say, and not for you," it is only a too finicky, only an absurd lawyer who would say, "I don't want to be your lawyer." If a client hasn't got the wisdom to be persuaded by a persuasive lawyer, that is the client's business. But I should like to emphasize this, because I think it is one of the gravest shortcomings of lawyers to be content to give their clients merely the advice of whether this is or is not within the law, this is or is not permitted, without making themselves the advisers or counselors of clients in dealing with everyday events.

So there is a grave responsibility on the individual lawyers, scattered all over the United States, to guide with wisdom and foresight beyond the appreciation of the preoccupied client who cannot see, because that isn't his business, the relevancies beyond the immediate situation.

That is not only a responsibility, but a very great satisfaction, and I should think, after considerable observation of lawyers but with little actual practical experience in advising clients, it must be one of the greatest satisfactions of a lawyer's life to guide his clients into channels of wisdom, into forbearance, even into generosities beyond the immediate requirements of the law.

To be a lawyer, merely a lawyer, not to be tempted to go into public office, not to have a temperament for public office, not to branch off into other temptations that come to lawyers, but to be a real practicing lawyer I think is a great calling.

I think of three great names in the history of our legal profession of men who were nothing but lawyers, who were clients' advisers, and real advocates and writers of private opinions for private clients throughout their long and fruitful and distinguished lives.

There was the famous lawyer in Massachusetts still arguing cases at ninety. He was Sidney Bartlett. When he died and there was a memorial meeting before the Supreme Judicial Court of Massachusetts, Mr. Justice Holmes, then Chief Justice of the Commonwealth, in response to a motion from the bar, said, "Our famous leader was content to remain to the close Mr. Bartlett of the Suffolk bar."

Contemporaneously, going beyond Bartlett's life, was the great lawyer who I suppose was the leading advocate when I came to the bar, John G. Johnson of Philadelphia. Certainly twice, and I think three times he was asked to go on the Supreme Court. Three times Presidents had asked him, and wanted to appoint him to the Supreme Court bench, and he declined because he preferred the life of the advising lawyer, with a vast range of responsibilities to his private clients.

He was given to blunt talk. When his friends said to him, "Well, why don't you go on the Supreme Court?" he said, "You finally want me to tell you the true reason? I would rather talk to those damn fools than listen to them!"

And still a third lawyer, the second lawyer to my knowledge who declined an appointment to the Supreme Court, who preferred to be a practicing lawyer—an ordinary lawyer, if you will—comes down almost to yesterday, and that was John W. Davis.

All those three men of great distinction, of great quality, of great culture, all three fit to be on the Supreme Court, preferred the activities, the responsibilities—and I repeat, to you, young men and young ladies—the satisfactions of guiding the difficult complexities, the onerous burdens of clients who need the advice of wise counsel.

And particularly is this true in our country, the United States of America, because of the nature of our political system: the fact that we are a federalism; the fact that, barring only the District of Columbia, over every foot of territory two governments exist with two sets of laws, with two sets of courts, and with sometimes conflicting, concurring, or diverging authority.

It is also true in England, that today we see law is pervasive, where everybody is governed, as the saying goes, from the cradle to the grave. It is true in England, but it is particularly true in this country, where two sets of governments administrate such a vast complex of laws from the cradle to the grave. Certainly it is not difficult to see and appreciate why the lawyer serves such an important function in our modern society.

Hardly any businessman, hardly any labor union, or any charitable organization can move without the need for direction, guidance, and finally—and I can't repeat it too often—the wisdom of those who are officers by virtue of being lawyers, who are the officers and the ministers of the law.

Look at the part that lawyers have played not only in past Anglo-American history, but in the everyday unfolding today of the myriad of matters that come under the heading of civil liberties, many of them enshrined within our Bill of Rights. Look at the part that lawyers have played in our democracy from the framing of the Constitution itself right down to our present day, and you cannot fail to appreciate the importance of your calling, and the full import of the duties that lie ahead of you.

It isn't accident, I think, that unlike the situation in the House of Commons, most of the membership of the House of Representatives, and of the Senate of the United States consists of lawyers, and that has been true from the beginning. No, the participation of lawyers in the framing of the Constitution was not accidental.

Take the most distinguished members on either the diplomatic side, or the service side of our government; it isn't accident that they are lawyers. It isn't accident that the first Secretary of State was so eminent a lawyer as Thomas Jefferson. It isn't accident that you find the men who followed him so frequently were lawyers. Those who stand out conspicuously as Secretaries of State, possibly with one exception, as far as I am concerned, were lawyers. It isn't accidental that the great Secretaries of War in the history of this country were lawyers. It isn't accidental.

During the war, a well known Frenchman, Jean Monnet, said to me one day, "Will you please explain to me why the men whom I regard as the most effective, the most fruitful, the most creative, are lawyers?" And perhaps in this household, I ought not to be too modest, and quote still another question of his, "And why are most of them Harvard Law School men?"

Well, I said I didn't think it was accident, and the reason is because, unlike France, with us almost every important question in the history of the United States is ultimately shaped for adjudication by the Supreme Court. Now when you have a situation such as that, a federated nation with an intricate legal system, there is an inevitable role for the lawyer that is not often true of other countries, and as I told my friend Monnet, the reason that that is so is because, on the whole, the training of the lawyer is to a great degree training for disinterested analysis not true to such degree in any other profession.

To see one side of a problem is easy. Almost everybody can do that. To see at least two, and as is often required, more than two sides, takes a special training found only in the legal profession. And in pride I say that in no place, in no law school in this country is the tradition of disinterested inquiry, instead of predetermined results, more dominant than in the Harvard Law School. Long may it remain so!

I see I have already exceeded the half hour during which I found myself, with pleasure, talking to you. I am a happy, captive speaker, but I could go on to indicate various other aspects in which the discipline, the training that you have enjoyed, or will enjoy at the end of three years, will, I hope, find you all truly disinterested in your approach, full of inquiry, and possessed of the ability to see a problem in its complicated entirety, not fragments of the problem—in the words of Justice Brandeis, become counsel for the total situation.

There are diverse ways in which those things will come to you, but it is my wish that you too, like the three men I mentioned to you, Sidney Bartlett, John W. Davis, and John G. Johnson — or, my friend too early departed, Julius Amberg, who never would move out of Grand Rapids, Michigan, or a man who is in this room now, I think, and I don't see him so I don't see his blushes, who is spending the most fruitful and full life in service as a practicing lawyer—it is my wish that you will all become true counselors of the law and not allow yourselves to be sidetracked from rendering service in a manner that is true to your profession. Of course, some of you will be lured into industry; many men are. But why do so many of them come through the law?

I asked a brilliant product of this School about that, Robert Page, when he became head of Phelps-Dodge, one of the biggest industrial enterprises in the land. He came in to see me after that took place, and I said, "Bob, by what impudence do you allow yourself to become president of Phelps-Dodge Company? What qualifications have you got? You don't know anything about geology." He said, "I boned up on the terms, and the qualification for the head of a great industry is the capacity to ask the right questions of the technicians, of the experts."

I hope that you will not all want to become presidents of these big enterprises, because I can assure you, expressing the feelings of many, many men in the profession, I can assure you, the greatest satisfaction will come in the practice of the law, and the ways in which legal activities will unfold in your futures.

If a Justice of the Supreme Court had been here while I was a member of the student body, in my old Austin Hall —I should like to have been told not what I said, but what I am trying to say, what Justice Holmes said after years of doubt—it took him years to discover, despite his intellect and abstract intellectual yearnings, to find satisfaction in the law. And too many people forget that he too did hard grubbing in the law from the time he got out until he went to the Supreme Judicial Court in 1882.

I want to say, if I had been in the seats then as you are now, I would have wanted to be told not what I said but the indications that I have tried to give, that you belong to a profession with a great tradition, a tradition which you must continue, not as an inert heritage, but through your own efforts an ever-continuing heritage of service. Yes, you belong to a profession that is indispensable to the well-being of our society which has its joys, its difficulties, its burdens, as do all human activities. But it also has satisfactions which you will find in your rendering of service and help to other men, satisfactions that can come only from enlarging the vision of society while maintaining its great past.

MR. FREUND: And now to those of you who plan to be corporation executives, and others, may you ask the right questions.

JUSTICE FRANKFURTER: Let's decide on the terminal period. I don't think the elders ought to be allowed to talk. I was told that it would be highly desirable if I should open myself up to your cross-examination. I won't disclose the naïve creature who said that, but it was one of the members of the faculty. I would say only this, I will either try to answer every question in the time allowed, or tell you why I don't answer it.

FROM THE FLOOR: I wonder if you would comment on Professor Hart's article in the *Harvard Law Review*.[1]

JUSTICE FRANKFURTER: I see you got the innuendo of my remark. Oh how I wish I still occupied a chair instead of a seat on the bench. How I would love to tell you of that part with which I agreed, and that which I would like to cross-examine him on. I do not want to talk about any matters connected with the Supreme Court. I do not like to give mutilated or partial comments. I don't like to comment on things as to which I cannot fully lay bare my mind. I cannot deal with Professor Hart's article without going into the life of the Supreme Court. I would like to be around here a hundred years from now and see the comments that are made about the present life of the Supreme Court, but, since it is still in existence, I think I will have to defer to history on that subject. I cannot talk about any of these things. Some other things I have talked about in opinions, and I assume, of course, students read the opinions of the Supreme Court, even though their professors may not.

But I cannot talk for instance about the whole problem of the FELA cases without going outside of the bounds for one in my position, so that takes care of all questions regarding the segregation issue. And for a very good reason.

[1] Henry M. Hart, Jr., "The Time Chart of the Justices," *Harvard Law Review* 73:84 (November 1959).

Let me add further, I do not think any member of the Supreme Court should talk about contemporaneous decisions. Because of the nature of the adversary process, an adjudication should be made on the basis of argument to come before the Court in a particular case. And comments by a member of the Court on these opinions, in public or in private, of what an opinion may mean are, from my point of view, hostile to the full play of the adversary process of the Supreme Court adjudication.

FROM THE FLOOR: You told us of many of the satisfactions, would you tell us about some of the doubts that we might experience, and how in your opinion, they may be overcome?

JUSTICE FRANKFURTER: In the first place, lawyers had better remember they are human beings, and a human being who hasn't his periods of doubts and distresses and disappointments must be a cabbage, and not a human being. That is number one.

Judge Learned Hand once said to me, "The next time I am born, I don't want to be a lawyer. I don't want to be doing what I am doing, judging these cases." I said, "What would you like to be?" He said, "I think I would like to be a biologist, or biochemist." I said, "You know a number of eminent scientists. Ask them how many times they make experiments in their laboratories, how many days or weeks they spend, and sometimes months, and the upshot result is negative?"

Well, grubbing through digests, reading the opinions of some Supreme Courts, not merely those of the Supreme Court of the United States, is not the most edifying form of literature that I can think of, but those are the materials, the raw materials out of which you are to gain the tools of your profession. A scientist may take ten years making tests and tests, in pursuit of some idea and eventually he thinks he may establish it. I am not suggesting, and I hope there is no inference in anything I have said that suggests that the profession of the law is a bed of roses.

I am not suggesting that at all. I am saying that when you count the doubts, the difficulties, the boredom, the repetitiveness, the obtuse clients—and obtuse judges, if you will—when you get through with all that, on the other side you overbalance the debits with the satisfactions; that is, if you have the appropriate temperament you will be on solid ground.

Holmes once said law is the profession of thinkers, not of artists. On more than one occasion I have had friends, fathers whose sons were here, and the sons wanted to be lawyers because their fathers wanted them to be. Of course, that kind of pressure by fathers upon sons isn't always direct or concrete. The atmosphere is created whereby the son having a happy time with his father would like to practice law with him. But sometimes by temperament the son wasn't meant to be a lawyer. On the whole there are people who by temperament do not like the disputatious process of the law, the fine distinctions, the nice discriminations, who don't care what they call a thing. "Oh, that is all folderol, all verbal." The instruments of the law are words. If you are of that temperament, if nature meant you to be a painter, for God's sake, don't become a lawyer; but be sure that nature meant you to be a painter, and a decent one.

FROM THE FLOOR: Sir, on the qualifications of a good law teacher, and good practicing lawyer, are they the same, or do they differ? Would you care to characterize the difference?

JUSTICE FRANKFURTER: No, I don't think they are the same. I don't think they are exclusive. I don't think it is an either/or thing. I haven't any doubt that if Professor Scott had remained in New York, I haven't the slightest doubt, by any standard, that he would be one of the most successful lawyers at the bar. It was by one of those contingencies on which so much of life turns that Dean Ames died and Scotty was asked to come up here and fill out the year, and he found teaching very interesting, very provocative, very satisfying, and he was asked to stay, and he did stay.

Now you have got there a prime example, from my point of view, one who just would have been without question a first-class lawyer, and he became a pre-eminent teacher. But some people who like the processes of the law, who like the problems of the law, don't like the practicalities of spending hours in the details of a client's business. There are those who prefer merely the intellectual processes. Law is, by its nature, involved in intellectual processes, but the practice of law involves a lot of other things, and there are men who by temperament don't like that aspect of the practice.

Vice versa, there are other men. I have in mind one of the most eminent products of this School, Joseph P. Cotton, who would have been a great teacher, or a great anything for that matter, who was several times called here and wouldn't come because he preferred the practice of law, and afterwards became Under Secretary of State in the Hoover Administration.

I could pass on the advice that I received when I was confronted with the question of leaving private practice and going to the United States Attorney's office. I wrote to Dean Ames, whom I revered and still revere, asking for his help, and for his advice, for his illumination, and he wrote back in his own handwriting, "I am sure if you join Mr. Stimson's staff, you will give him satisfaction, as I am sure you will be very happy to serve under him. As to what to do, follow the dominant impulses of your career. Sincerely yours, James Barr Ames." Well, that didn't tell me which road to take. But as life became more intelligible to me, I thought, and I still think it was profoundly wise advice that he gave me.

After all, we are dealing with mature men, even though they are in their twenties. There is something inside—I suppose what Socrates called the inner voice—which if you reflect long enough will say "practice is for you," "teaching is for you." It doesn't follow that you will be a successful practitioner, or successful teacher. I know that is very vague, but that is the vague advice Dean Ames gave me, and I still think it is profound advice.

FROM THE FLOOR: Mr. Justice, I was advised that you had advised that when a student starts out wondering where he should practice, he should start with the presumption he should go back to his home town, or at least locally. If I have quoted you correctly, I wonder if you might comment on that.

JUSTICE FRANKFURTER: May you never be more wrong. I ought to say, after saying that is my view, what my wife thinks. While I expressed those views to students during all the happy years that I was here, she said I was taking a lot of liberty with young lives, because the only small towns I ever knew anything about were Vienna, New York, and Boston.

Now, barring that, I think, number one, it is a great mistake to believe that there is no full life except in a great big metropolis, in a great big city. When I hear men say, as I have heard them say, "Oh, Denver is so small, Buffalo is so small," I say to them, "Yes, New York is so big." They say, "Look at all the opportunities of New York. There is something going on every day of the musical season. There are not less than twelve concerts to go to.

There is the Metropolitan Opera House." I say, "Ask your friends how often they go to the Metropolitan."

Secondly—I have mentioned in my opening remarks that Julius Amberg was one of the most gifted lawyers; he stood out among lawyers. He never would leave Grand Rapids, Michigan, but he didn't practice in Grand Rapids. He practiced all over his state. He is another illustration of a fellow who wanted to remain a lawyer. He was asked to be Attorney General of Michigan. He didn't want that. He was asked to go on the Supreme Court of Michigan. He didn't want that. He got fulfillment in practicing in Grand Rapids.

Finally, I think it is a terribly bad thing for the country if its dominant talent is concentrated in a few cities. On the whole, in your own community where you have your roots and connections the presumption is that you must answer to yourself just why you don't want to go back there. At least that is what my wife would call my purely academic, impractical point of view.

FROM THE FLOOR: Just what would you think might be a good way by which the bar could improve what might be called its public image with the laity?

JUSTICE FRANKFURTER: Well, in the first place, what you call the laity image of the bar I would not take too seriously, because that is always with us. Dean Pound was fond of saying that Jack Cade hates us; the first thing he would do when he got into power is cut off the heads of lawyers. People who know they need you are simply having a little fun at your expense, but that doesn't mean that they don't value the bar.

In the second place, and this I haven't said, and I thank you for the question. The citizen shouldn't be lost in the lawyer. I do not think it is necessary for a man to enter public life to contribute to public life. But I have said, and

I say it again, to my mind, in a democracy, in our society the most important office is the citizen. And the lawyer has a very special responsibility as a citizen, in giving guidance through speeches, letters to the press—not hot-air talk at bar associations about how wonderful we are—but guidance, and illumination on public issues. To a large extent I think it is true in many parts of this country the lawyers have an influence over the community far beyond what is true of them in the big cities where everybody is so merged in the mass.

There are no short cuts to any of these things. You must exercise citizenship in the way which it comes to you to exercise it, through talking with people, at luncheons, at your club. If you really know what you are talking about, people will listen. I am a great believer in Emerson's lovely wisdom that somehow people find their way to the best—what is it—mousetrap! If you are addressing a city club, or a union meeting, and are talking sense, they will go away reflecting on it. They want to hear what you have to say the next time a question comes up.

No, there aren't any patent medicines. I don't know what their function has been in medicine—probably very dubious, but there are certainly no patent medicines in the field of politics in the large sense, government or society generally.

FROM THE FLOOR: Would you comment on the caliber of oral advocacy that you see before you at the bench?

JUSTICE FRANKFURTER: Not with joy, but with sadness. It is on the whole really not very good. And I will tell you why it isn't very good. Because on the whole most lawyers do not qualify in regard to the first item on which I commented; namely, they are really not cultivated lawyers. I have said to myself often, as I listened to these arguments, I would give a good cookie to know what this fellow has read during the last three years, besides *Time*, *Life*, and the higher flight of that category, *Fortune*. When I read the briefs, similar thoughts occur to me. It is seldom that I have occasion to come home and tell my wife it was really enjoyable to listen to an argument today.

And might I say on this occasion, on this point, I don't think it is my prejudice that leads me to say that certainly some of the best arguments that we hear come from what might be called obscure lawyers from small towns. As a case is called, and counsel get on their feet, the pages put on the desks of each of us the name and city. Again and again I send for the postal guide to find out the population of the town from which that fellow comes, and again and again I am surprised at the quality of argument from lawyers from small towns.

Now I don't draw any great big generalization from that. I merely offer it to you as a fact. I don't know what law schools can do about that. I remember when I was here, Mr. Justice Brandeis wrote me, "Isn't there something more that the Law School could do in improving the quality, the habits of mind of lawyers that appear before the courts? The arguments should be better."

Are there any men here from Pennsylvania in the audience? Well, John [John G. Buchanan, '12, of Pittsburgh], I don't want to reduce the modesty of your bar by telling you what I am about to tell you, as bearing on the quality of arguments and quality of briefs. But one day I had a note from Justice Brandeis saying, "Can you tell me, can you account for what I believe to be a fact, that on the whole, the best arguments that the Court has had since I have been on it have come from Pennsylvania lawyers?" Many years passed, and he discovered that the rules of the Supreme Court of Pennsylvania require that the question to be argued has to be stated separately, no matter how brief the question, on a separate page of the brief. It is done that way so that you will really know what point you are talking about.

And in the second place, there is a rule. What is your rule, John?

MR. BUCHANAN: Thirty minutes, no matter how much time the Court takes.

JUSTICE FRANKFURTER: This is not a prearranged dialogue. I want you to have it authoritatively from Mr. Buchanan. Under the Pennsylvania rule the argument is limited to thirty minutes, and as he said unappreciatively, the judges may take part of that.

And Justice Brandeis said that it was his opinion that that necessity for formulating the issue conspicuously on a page all by itself, and the necessity of hoarding your time because you haven't got any more, make for greater effort and greater clarity, and greater relevance in the argument.

And I might add it was very great good fortune for many years, too few alas, to sit next to the man on the court who was without doubt the most experienced and most distinguished advocate, before he had come on the court, of anybody in my time, barring only Chief Justice Hughes, Mr. Justice Jackson, who was an advocate of absolutely the first order.

We exchanged many views as the arguments went on, and we both agreed that the best arguments we get are in cases on what is called the summary docket, in which only a half an hour is allowed to counsel. If you have only a half an hour, you can't afford to waste most of it in spreading yourself. A number of lawyers think it is a constitutional duty to use an hour when they have got it.

FROM THE FLOOR: Mr. Justice, it has been said that the private practice of law is dying out. Do you lament this trend, or do you think it is a good thing?

JUSTICE FRANKFURTER: I don't believe it, and if it were true, I would deplore it.

FROM THE FLOOR: You mentioned to us a few of the names of people who seem to have inspired you. Could you tell us some of the others?

JUSTICE FRANKFURTER: Oh, I would have to mention almost every member of the Harvard Law School faculty when I was a student. By the way, I should have mentioned another man—I don't know if he was formally asked, but I know he indicated that he would not accept a Supreme Court appointment, and that was my chief, Mr. Stimson, who, of course, had an extraordinary and distinguished career. But he said that private practice to him was something that he would always cherish, despite his ventures and successes in public life. I suppose he was the only man who was a member of the Cabinet of four Presidents. He said it was comforting to know that there was always the haven of his old law firm to which he could return after he successfully left one public office after another. He said that that was a source of comfort while he was in public office, that he wasn't dependent upon that office entirely, that he had a great calling that he could go to if for some reason or another the uncertainties of public life made it appropriate for him to leave it.

And I think that the young men who want to go into public office right away, assuming they are meant to be lawyers, should bear that well in mind and not give all their attention to political fortune, which too often is misfortune.

FROM THE FLOOR: You spoke of the cultural outlook necessary for the law. Do you think the law schools should do more than they are doing now with the increasing complexities of law?

JUSTICE FRANKFURTER: Well, you are talking to a fellow with strong views on this subject. I don't think the law school can be a substitute for, or make up for the lack of college, let alone high school. I think if the law school has a sufficiently eminent faculty, as I believe this Law School has, and has had, and, I hope, will continue to have, then every law professor ought to generate in his classrooms a realization that you must not merely restrict yourself to cases that are assigned, or other reading matter that is assigned.

The limitations of the lawyer, and the reason why lawyers are not wise in their advice, often is that, on the whole, men are drawn to law because they haven't got the imagination which the arts require. Art is the domain of the imagination, whether poet, painter or sculptor, composer or conductor. But since the imagination deals with perceptions that are not as translatable into specific detailed terms, it is up to the lawyer to regard it as a function and even duty to cultivate the limited imagination that we lawyers have. And how do you cultivate the imagination? Through the arts, by hearing good music and by looking at pictures, and reading great works of literature.

It is now past the hour. I thank you very much, and I assure you, as I come back here, I get reinvigorated and refreshed in the kind of things that this School means to you, and has always been to me.

To Members of The Council and The Faculty

JUSTICE FRANKFURTER: If I address you as beneficiaries, all, of the Harvard Law School, of course I include without formal mention Mr. Fowler, President Pusey, Dean Griswold, and Mr. Carrington.

I knew that I would be called upon to say a few words tonight, and of course I reflected somewhat on what to say, but I made a great mistake in such preparation as I did make in the chambers of my mind. Being a great believer in the importance of immediacy of communication between speaker and audience, I thought I could trust myself tonight, as I usually do, to be able to speak both out of mind and heart without having the heart overwhelm the mind.

But as I listened to what has been said, and as I thought of the whole occasion, that I myself should be the witness of what has been said and what has been thought about me, and considering the feelings I have about this institution, and my own sense of diffidence in any kind of personal communication, I said to myself, I wish I had the courage, if it was courage, of Professor Pavlov, the world-renowned physiologist, whom a scientific friend of mine thought it would be educative for me just to look upon, even if with total incapacity of understanding, when he came here during the physiological world conference held at Harvard. He was introduced in terms of—what shall I say—in terms praising his scientific significance, certainly more true than all the wonderful things that have been said here tonight, by one of the great figures of the Harvard of those days, Dr. Walter Cannon, who set forth the personal achievements of this great world figure in the domain of physiological science.

And when Professor Pavlov rose to deliver his address, I thought it was one of the most wonderful experiences for me of the true function of self-indifference, which ought to be one of the outstanding characteristics of a scholar, that Professor Pavlov made not one word of reference to what was said about him, but immediately went to the blackboard and began to draw some diagrams and at once held forth on the paper which he was delivering.

Well, I am not sure that it would be courage on my part if I followed his example. I think it would be the height of ungraciousness. It would be a form of self-consciousness even greater than the self-consciousness which possesses me at this moment. And so all I can say is that although this is a homecoming, as Dean Griswold wrote me it would be when I told him of the ordeal to which I looked forward, although it is a homecoming, I can assure you, never did I feel so ill at ease at a family party in my life.

President Pusey, I think you are the one person in this gathering, unless I am mistaken, who cannot through personal experience but merely through the osmosis which a president of a university comes to acquire, *ex officio*, appreciate the sense of reverence—I put it no lower—the sense of reverence which fills, I am sure, most of us in this room, and the alumni generally of this Law School, about this institution.

I can assure you that reverence is an accurate description, an accurate concept with which to indicate my own feeling about this institution.

I came here as a lad fifty-seven years ago, almost fifty-seven years ago, and almost throughout my first year, I was the scaredest kid that you can imagine. For two reasons.

In the first place, I marvelled at the audacity of men in the class who began to pipe up almost the second day after they had arrived at the School. And when I contemplate that they did so in a class in which Samuel Williston, the great Williston, was the teacher, I really had a streak of yellow in me asserting itself, from which only fear saved me from saying, "This is too fast a team for me, and I better go back to New York."

It took me a whole year to get over that feeling. I think it is a fact that I hardly—despite this bit of history that President Pusey dug up of my talking—I don't think I spoke up at all during the course of the first year.

And when that fatal envelope came during the summer with the marks from the Harvard Law School—the outside envelope indicated that it was from the Harvard Law

School—with a cowardly feeling, it took me minutes before I dared open that envelope to see what the result was.

Mr. Carrington nods—I am sure that has been the experience of all except those who somehow or other divine that they are really meant for greatness in the law. Well, that may be described as predominantly a feeling of awe, and I was awed during that first year. The awe was transmuted, and has become, and is reverence.

What was there about it that should evoke such a feeling, an almost religious term about a secular institution like this? I suppose ultimately it is the quality of men under whom I had the good fortune to study and those of my time, a few of whom I see about me. My beloved classmate Robert Miller is happily here. It is the quality of men who were our teachers.

I was much interested in Mr. Fowler saying that the law has—I thought it was rather an extraordinary use of the word—even the law has spiritual values.

Well, how could you escape spiritual values, if that word has not been misused? How could you escape feeling that you were in the presence of something pure, something noble, something dedicated, in being a participant in one of those classes? That is what it was, a participant in the enterprise of the dedicated endeavor to understand, without any prepossessions, without any starting points of conscious bias, however you may be unwittingly biased. How could you escape having such feelings stirred in you and permanently lodged in you, when your teachers were James Barr Ames, Samuel Williston, Jeremiah Smith, John Chipman Gray, Joseph Henry Beale, to mention the predominant ones, numerically predominant members of the faculty at the time? Is it any wonder we were inspired, having the good fortune to be guided by such dedicated men? Indeed there were spiritual values prevailing in this atmosphere.

And so we left the Law School permanently infused with the feeling that there is about the law the application of reason to purposeful ends—and one does not use words too lightly—at least an ideal and aim dedicated and erected toward noble ends: the adjustment through law of inevitable conflicts among men, poor fallible creatures; the adjustment of their interacting conflicts, of the confusion of their purposes, of misunderstanding of their so-called best interests, the settlement of those conflicts and interactions and contradictions through a process of reasoning.

I should mention—I am sorry I omitted him—not one of the most—what shall I say—dramatic characters of those days, but a teacher to whom I am deeply indebted, as indeed are most of us who had the good fortune to sit under him in small classes, particularly in his own private tea classes, as it were, Professor Wambaugh.

Well, and so the School sent us out with that kind of feeling not merely about the School; we carried the irradiating influence of those men into the world outside. There was a dominance of trying to understand, of trying to pierce difficulties, of tearing off the outward wrappings, of seeing the complications beneath the simplicities of the surface and, contrariwise, the simplicities between apparently muddled complexities under the surface.

And here I am tonight, compelled, graciously compelled, to listen to things said about me, joining me with people about whom I felt as I have just tried to explain. And when the School asked me to join the faculty, a request that came out of a clear sky, I remember saying at the time, I could not have been more surprised if I had had an invitation from an East Indian princess to marry her.

Mr. President, it may interest you to know, since the significance of a university derives from the quality and the constant stream of the kind of scholars whom you sketched and delineated—it may interest you to know that when I was asked to join the faculty, and I made inquiry whether I had to make a prompt answer, or could take my time, it was so unexpected, so sudden a choice or an opportunity, at all events an offer with which I was confronted, I was told I could take my time. I remember—believe me, it was true—I debated back and forth whether I should go back and practice law with Mr. Stimson—I had just finished service with him in his first Secretaryship of War—or whether I should come here.

I talked to Mr. Justice Brandeis about this, before he was Mr. Justice Brandeis. He said, "What are the difficulties in your mind? Why do you hesitate?" I said, the decisive reason why I pause and hesitate, my greatest feeling that I ought not to do it is that I cannot think of myself in terms of the faculty of the Harvard Law School who were my teachers.

It is just that I could not think of myself fit for the company of men like Ames and Gray, and Williston, and Beale. And Thayer, who died, unfortunately, just before I came here. Mr. Wambaugh always said I would have found him the most sympathetic of all teachers. I just couldn't think of myself as satisfying the kind of qualities that those men had permanently embedded in me as requisite for membership in the faculty of this School.

Why do I say that? Because if there is one quality which should control and guide and dominate a teacher, it is complete disinterestedness; you may have a better term for it, but I mean that exclusion of biases, and prepossessions, and prejudices, to the extent that you are aware of them—you can't exclude them entirely—we are all products of our time, all products of our antecedents. You can control them at least through awareness, and give them, so far as you can do so, their proper weight, or proper discounts in the ultimate judgment. I suppose the scholar, the teacher, certainly, of course, the scholar in the law, if he has one guiding function, if there is one virtue about which there should be no question, it is disinterestedness.

And therefore, to that extent, of course, the judge is akin to the scholar, with limitations and qualifications, because the professor, the scholar, need make no intellectual compromise. We all, as human beings, make compromises but the scholar in his classroom need make no compromise. If he is a scholar he can express his views without thinking whether somebody else agrees with him or not, whether it is wise in this particular instance to express his disagreement, or whether there is an institutional claim upon his thinking which subordinates expressed differences of opinions to what may be deemed a more important functional good. No such consideration must influence the scholar in his classroom. And to that extent—but only to that extent —in my opinion, is the judge not akin to the scholar.

And so it was that when friends of the Boston bar—some being glad to have me go to Washington for one reason, some for another—when they gave me a farewell party before I went to Washington—and I had to say a few words, I said this: That in going to this new task of mine, to this new activity in the law, I should like to be judged as a judge by the standards and the criteria by which members of the Harvard Law School are to be judged in their work of scholarship. I said that then, more than twenty-one years ago, and I say it tonight, subject to the limitation that while a scholar is an exclusive, self-contained, self-directing, self-defining individual, it is not true of a judge.

I do not mean to say that a judge should defer to the convictions of other people. I do say there are times when the judge should pocket his disagreement and decide whether a particular thing is so important as against certain institutional considerations, or the force and authority of the judgment of the court, not always to whistle his own tune.

That, President Pusey—and I address you in particular, as one who for this occasion has been adopted into the fraternity, into the fellowship of lawyers,—that gives you my general view, and perhaps the least—what shall I say—heart-overwhelming comment that I can make about the things that have been said about me in the course of this dinner.

That my name should ever be coupled with the names of those I have mentioned tonight would have seemed a strange emanation of a diseased brain fifty years ago, and even tonight it sounds like fanciful talk.

I come back to this School always with a sense of—what shall I say—"take off thy shoes, for this is holy ground." I come back to this place always with a sense of homage, and gratitude, active, dynamic, creative, functioning gratitude insofar as the power within me lies.

I ought not to sit down without saying a word—I said some words, a good many words this afternoon—about our profession, to the young over in Austin Hall.

But in this gathering I have some other remarks to make about our profession, speaking to those who already share and have shared some of the responsibilities of the profession. And I see among you many lawyers of importance throughout the country in your various activities and your various opportunities, important functionaries of the law, and I would like to say something, first about the profession as I see its responsibilities in the future, and a final word about the Law School in respect to it.

The Germans with true arrogance used to talk, even in pre-Hitlerian days, about their *Rechtsstaat*. They thought they were the legal state. Well, I think that no society, no nation, is a *Rechtsstaat*, or a law state, to the extent that the

United States is, for the reasons I told the boys this afternoon—or did I? I meant to. We are a federal society, with all the complexities, with all the challenges to resourcefulness, with all the demands upon ingenuity and tolerance and understanding and breadth of vision that a society within a federalism demands. But especially is this true of this country, because of those features in our Constitution to which there is no parallel in any of the other federal constitutions, neither Australia, Canada, nor India, with a constitution that was patterned in many ways after intensive study of our workings upon our own Constitution.

I refer, of course, to those vague, undefined, indefinable provisions of our Constitution which give rise to our greatest difficulties, those majestic provisions of due process of law and equal protection of the laws. The application of those clauses, and the function of the lawyer, and not merely of the Supreme Court as the ultimate arbiter, to me become increasingly difficult and demanding as our society becomes more and more interrelated, as the division of political functions between states and nation more and more calls for nice distinctions, and for final tolerances.

Every public speaker these days talks about the challenge that confronts this country, and we can all agree that the fact of the challenge cannot be overstated. Whence comes the challenge?

It isn't merely the East-West situation. It isn't merely what so glibly falls from the lips of speakers on the challenge of Russia. I believe if there had continued to be a Czarist regime we would in many ways have had much of the challenge that is now confronting us, for the simple reason that the great changes in the world which have taken place have greatly affected the relation of this country to the rest of the world and within our country, with our classes, and sections and divisions.

We must, as Lincoln said at the time of the Civil War, "disenthrall ourselves" of a lot of old notions. The dominant notion, down to the Spanish War and certainly after the first World War, let alone the second, was that this was "God's country." This was God's own country! Here was a vast, virgin continent to be exploited; with the great benefits that this exploitation would bring about, the development of this country could take place in a society with a mobility possessed by no other nation in the world. Society can move within the democratic framework with the least obstruction because of the mobility of society, not only the physical mobility, the constant westward flow, but also social mobility within each section of the society.

One doesn't have to go into the contested historical controversy about the frontier and its influence. The fact of the matter is that it has had an important influence. This was God's country because here we were, selected to have these benefits of nature with the human capacity, the enterprise of our people, because of our mobility, to take advantage of these natural opportunities. And we assumed that that was the great gift of nature, even to the extent that we were guarded by two great oceans—there they were—great ramparts protecting us. (Most people forget that there was also a British Navy that took care of our needs.)

All that has gone. Not only that, but the whole idea of transmitting democracy into real meaning, not only political democracy but individual fulfillment by every member of the community, has brought forth problems of great difficulty, but also of majesty.

And then, also, this free development involves the whole relation between what is summarily called capital and labor. I read the other day two fat but interesting volumes, the life of Benjamin Harrison, a vague figure in my mind until I read this. From this life I derived a vivid sense of the kind of red lights that were shown on the landscape in the seventies and eighties, to which hardly anybody paid any attention, really serious industrial conflicts which were disposed of, or, rather, not disposed of, in ways that begot great trouble for the future.

Now, what has all this to do with the lawyer? It has a great deal to do with the lawyer.

I remember running into, by chance meeting, Mr. James Byrne, a most happy memory to all of us who knew him, a great figure at the bar and a valued member of the Corporation before your days, President Pusey, and in the life of this School. He was a man of considerable wealth, and the adviser of great wealth, as most of you know. I ran into him as my wife and I were leaving the Ritz in Boston. We were going home for an appropriately austere professor's dinner, and up came Mr. Byrne. And I had known him. From him came the first professional income I ever earned, I started as a clerk in his office, and the last salary that I drew from this university also came from Mr. Byrne; I was the holder of the first Byrne Professorship. He stopped us and said, "Where are you going?" And the upshot was that we sat down and had dinner together, and this was in the middle of the 1936 campaign. And we talked about this and that, and we talked about the various enactments, the Securities Act, and so on, and so forth. And I asked him what he thought about all this business —the New Deal legislation. And he said—I think he would have shocked most of his friends in Wall Street if they had heard him—he said, "I haven't a particle of doubt that much of this legislation is hasty and shallow, and not thoroughly thought through, but who am I to criticize President Roosevelt for urging these measures, or for signing them, or Congress for passing them, when he had

—overnight practically—to correct evils that for fifty years we left unattended in the hope and the assumption that, somehow or other, all of these difficulties would straighten themselves out."

I think that is an excellent example of what I mean by the bar's responsibility. My friend Paul Freund and his associates are writing a history of the Supreme Court. I hope one of these days some of your scholars, President Pusey, will be writing of the responsibility of the bar, as inadequate advisers of amenable clients, for many of the evils that have been allowed to gather only to be dealt with, too often—as Mr. Byrne said, cleaning up messes that have gathered for fifty years—by cleaning them up overnight.

I told the students this afternoon what I so strongly feel, that again and again and again I listen to arguments before the Court on controversial constructions of this statute or that—nice, fine casuistic reasoning, and one side delights in that as much as the other—without regard to the wisdom or the right or wrong of a particular conduct, but insistence that what was done by an enterprise was right because the law allowed it. Again and again I say to myself, and sometimes to a hospitable ear either to the left or right of me, "Why didn't this lawyer, in advising his client, consider beyond construction, whether it is right or wise?"

As I told the boys this afternoon, only last Thursday, in a matter of great importance, a controversy was engendered because a lawyer had said that this particular business can do thus and so, when it would not have mattered the slightest in the conduct of that business, if the lawyer had said, "You can do it, but you would be a damned fool if you did."

I could give endless illustrations of that because they have been deeply etched in my mind, as I sit up on that bench and listen to people stand on abstract rights without considering the consequences of the assertion of those rights.

I think controversies of such a kind, implied in that remark, will not lessen in the future. I would be greatly surprised if they would. And if I were to live as long as Mr. Burlingham, I would be indeed curious—I would like to be here and have people tell me whether in the course of the next twenty-five years, these conflicts, these frictions, these misunderstandings will be lessened and require less courageous, forthright wisdom for adjustment rather than the mere determination of legal right and legal wrong. Because legal right and legal wrong, after all, on the whole, are the minima of morality, and minima of social duties, and not the maxima of wisdom.

I think of things like the Mooney case: for twenty years, the State of California was in the throes of conflict over a man being locked up in San Quentin, convicted of a dreadful multiple murder, throwing of a bomb into a parade in 1916 in San Francisco.

Everybody thought it was terrible, when the State Department informed the present Governor of California that some South American governments were interested in the fate of a fellow awaiting execution. One of our leading Senators thought the official should be fired because an Assistant Secretary dispatched a note from a country with which we have friendly diplomatic relations—that was deemed an outrageous intervention of the State Department in local affairs.

Well, in the case of Mooney, it was President Wilson, over his own signature, in his own person, who intervened with the then Governor of California and said international relations were such that he wanted him to consider the situation. Well, Mooney was incarcerated for twenty years after it was established, demonstrated I think beyond a doubt (Archbishop Hanna told me at the time, "Tom Mooney is a bad man, but he didn't do that") that when he was convicted, the chief witness was a demonstrated perjurer. For twenty years this went on, but if six leading members of the California bar had given the governor the support and the strength and the authority of saying, "Do let him go," that would have been accepted, such is the strength of the bar. When I said to a friend of mine who was a leader of the bar, "Why don't you fellows do that?" he, being a canny Scot and witty man to boot, said, "Well, I will take that in hand on one condition. If you let me say to the governor that he can parole Mooney in your care!"

I could deal with a number of current problems where I think lawyers could be a little less concerned, lest they—what is it called—stick out their necks. I don't see why it is so terrible; why is it so terrible to stick out your neck? Or that thing which seems less reprehensible, to go out on a limb—many a limb is stout!

And this brings me to the School, Dean Griswold. Having indicated or sketched, or intimated the kind of demands I make upon my profession—President Pusey is quite right in saying, or indicating, he thinks we are an idolatrous profession—I think the basis for that feeling on his part is because too many idolatrous speeches are made at bar associations.

But having the feeling about the bar—not one of self-satisfaction, not one of glory, but of responsibility, I should like to say a word about the bearing of that on the function in the future of this School.

When I came to this School as a student, at that time, and for some years later, there was no school of comparable significance. It was true of this School in relation to law, as was true of Johns Hopkins in relation to medicine. It was first without competition.

And what has happened in medicine has happened in law. And, of course, we should be very happy about it because of the needs of the country—our relation to law, and our demands upon law would be ill-served if there were only one first-class law school.

I tell anxious parents, friends of mine who come and worry about their sons because, for one reason or another, they don't want to go to Harvard Law School. Where should a boy go? I answer, "If you will give me five minutes, I will rattle off the names of not less than twelve —and I might say a score of—very good law schools in this country," and I think we all ought to be very happy about that fact.

In a way, this School sent out missionaries. And the missionaries have established themselves in their own right all over the place. And we should be very grateful for that.

But I think we ought never surrender the conviction that there must be one place—the word "leadership" was used tonight; that is another word that is so often ill-used—we ought never surrender the conviction that there must be one place which deems it its special function to have a faculty of such quality, and to have purposes of such pre-eminence and preoccupation of such clarity, that there will be, despite the fact that there are many good law schools, a center of preeminent distinction; that experiments will be made here not because they are made in other places, but because they are not made in other places; that this School will be charging itself with self-conscious responsibilities, not of ancient preeminence—everybody wants to be first, or most people do—but because there is a need, despite the many outposts all over the place, the many good law schools, there is a need for a school which charges itself with being a pacemaker: a forerunner, a preoccupier of important neglected problems, an achiever of work of great distinction, of greater significance than is true of any other place.

And this of course gets back to President Pusey's demand. He stated the problem; I was hoping he would indicate how to approximate its achievement. Of course that gets back to his desire to have a succession of really great men as members of the faculty of this Law School.

I think great teachers, great scholars, partly become available because there are great scholars and great teachers already on the spot. I think there are problems for this School, and of its relation to legal education and law, that didn't exist fifty years ago. If you have a faculty of only eight or ten, you ought to have preeminence at least in six out of eight, or seven out of ten, and I think that was true on the faculty that those of us in my time had the good fortune to enjoy.

I think when you get a school of the present dimensions, and still more, when you have all this proliferation of courses—they are not all to my liking, as some of my friends well know (we make a fetish of "seminars," thinking every teacher has to have a seminar)—you have problems and difficulties confronting Dean Griswold that did not confront Dean Ames.

It isn't for me to suggest what the answers to those difficulties are. And the last thing in the world that I want to imply is that there aren't men on this faculty today, and a goodly number, of whom students in the future, fifty years from now, will speak as I have spoken tonight of Dean Ames and his colleagues. I do say that bigness of faculty and size of school and proliferation of courses, responsiveness to the need of having a course on every subject under the sun, beget problems that raise issues regarding the implied difficulties that such a situation produces. I shall again quote Mr. Byrne.

I remember while on the faculty, a meeting of the Harvard Law School Association—some of you, I am sure, were present, shortly after the first World War—and lawyers felt there were a lot of new emerging subjects, and the School wasn't doing a thing about them. There was no course on this, no course on that, and no course on the other thing. The president of the Association recognized Mr. Byrne, and, with his red hair flaming, he strode down the aisle with a vigorous stride, and he said in effect, "I have now listened to enough of this nonsense that friends of mine have uttered in criticizing the curriculum and work of the Law School. They all speak from practical experience to these professors, and the Dean. Now what entitles us to speak in this manner? What is our experience relevant to the educational program of this School?

"I suppose I have as large a law office as anybody in the United States. I suppose I have a very nice, select list of clients. And what does it all amount to? It is this case and that case, and the other case. Who am I to be entitled to tell the men of the Harvard Law School, and faculty, what their curriculum should be, or what it shouldn't be?

"You and I are entitled to one thing. We are entitled to say to the Harvard Law School, it should have a faculty of preeminence and, so long as that is true, the rest must be left entirely in their hands."

I have thrown out intimations that some of my friends on the faculty are aware of and disapprove. But I want to end by saying that I am confident there are now on this faculty people about whom fifty years from now, those who, like me, have gone through a long professional life, perchance members of the Supreme Court then—why shouldn't there be several Justices from the Harvard Law School fifty years from now—will feel as men of my time feel about our old faculty. So long as this faculty will have a preponderant body of eminent men, the devotion of our alumni will be unabated. And you can get eminence in the future only because there is a preponderant body on the faculty now. Like produces like. As long as we have men of distinction in good numbers, no matter what anybody may say, even Justices of the Supreme Court, the future of Harvard Law School will be secure.

I end with a feeling of truly inexpressible appreciation because I am too overwhelmed by the things that have been said tonight, and the honor that you have done me. All I can say is that I hope that in whatever time is left to me, I will not be unworthy of this School.

XXIII

Benjamin Nathan Cardozo

Mr. Justice Frankfurter's justly renowned essay on Mr. Justice Holmes, first published in Supplement One of the *Dictionary of American Biography* (1944), is paired by this biographical sketch of Mr. Justice Cardozo, written in May 1960 and published in *Collier's Encyclopedia* (1962), V, 418–420.

BENJAMIN NATHAN CARDOZO was the seventy-fifth Justice to sit on the Supreme Court. Of these seventy-five, few, hardly more than a dozen, had commanding distinction whose creative influence survived their day. Cardozo undoubtedly was one of the twelve. Such enduring significance normally requires long service on the Court. Cardozo's achievement is unique in that he attained it in little over five years. Chief Justice Hughes authoritatively accounted for this very rare achievement when he said that "No judge ever came to this Court more fully equipped by learning, acumen, dialectical skill, and disinterested purpose. He came to us in the full maturity of his extraordinary intellectual power, and no one on this bench has ever served with more untiring industry or more enlightened outlook." (305 U.S. xxv.)

Cardozo's was essentially an inner life—a life of the mind and spirit. The externals of his life can be quickly summarized. He was born in New York City May 24, 1870, and died, on July 9, 1938, after a long illness following a heart attack and stroke, at the home of his intimate friend,

Chief Judge Irving Lehman of the New York Court of Appeals, in Port Chester, New York. He was the youngest son of Albert and Rebecca Nathan Cardozo, descendants of Sephardic Jews who had settled in New York prior to the American Revolution. It is a rather droll fact that the lad Cardozo was privately tutored by Horatio Alger, the writer of story books for boys, before entering Columbia College. He graduated at the age of nineteen; a year later he received a master's degree while attending Columbia Law School. After his admission to the bar in 1891, he devoted himself for twenty-two years exclusively to the practice of his profession, seeking no public office, a figure unknown to the general public. He was in the main a lawyer's lawyer, not merely in the sense of earning high esteem from his brethren, but in that his professional work was largely for other lawyers.

That so modest, retiring and sensitive a nature as Cardozo, a lawyer so wholly withdrawn from the limelight, should have been elected a judge may properly be accounted to the great credit of popular election of judges, even though it was the result of one of those periodic triumphs of virtue in the checkered history of New York City politics. Though elected to a court predominantly concerned with litigation, he was allowed little experience as a trial judge. Within six weeks the governor designated him as a temporary judge on the Court of Appeals, the highest appellate tribunal of the state. He did so at the request of all its judges. Shortly thereafter, in January 1917, he was appointed a regular member of the Court of Appeals to fill a vacancy, and in the autumn of that year he was elected for a full term of fourteen years on the nomination of both the major parties. In 1927 he was elected without opposition its Chief Judge.

Even before he became the court's head, the quality of his opinions added new lustre to a court that had had a distinguished past. As Chief Judge, he infused a quality into the court not unlike that of a great conductor in bringing out the potential best in other members of the orchestra. His own mastery of the law, its principles and rules and their history, his power in adapting the wisdom of the past to the needs of his time, the literary distinction with which he unfolded his legal reasoning made him one of the very few judges whose fame spread throughout the world of English-speaking law. He influenced the fruitful development of the English common law wherever its writ runs. While still on the New York Court of Appeals, where he sat for eighteen years, the legal profession and legal scholars everywhere acknowledged his rightful place among the judicial luminaries in the entire history of American law.

When Mr. Justice Holmes, the most learned and most philosophic-minded of judges, retired in 1932, President Hoover in naming Cardozo to Holmes' place did not so much choose Cardozo as ratify the country's selection, expressed in and out of Congress, by bar and laity, of Cardozo as the inevitable successor to Holmes.

As already indicated, Cardozo was not allowed to run the course in Washington. What is unparalleled in the history of the Supreme Court, is the impress he made on his judicial brethren during the less than six full terms that he served on the Court and the influence that he has left behind him. It has been said by some of our greatest Justices that it requires three or four years even for the most capable minds and the most experienced lawyers to be able to take the work of the Court in their stride, to acquire adequate understanding of its jurisdictional problems and not feel overburdened by the range and volume of its business. With uncommon rapidity Cardozo made the adjustment from preoccupation with the comparatively restricted problems of private litigation to the exacting demands of the very different major judicial problems that come before the Court. These concern the proper equilibrium between nation and states in our federal system and the adjustment of the conflicting claims between individual liberty and the interests of society. Immense legal learning, wide cultivation beyond the bounds of law, a serene outlook and a tolerant view of his fellow men without mistaking tolerance for fuzziness of thought, intellectual courage, and a purity of heart that assured the almost automatic exercise of the two most important faculties called for in a Justice—disinterestedness and humility—equipped Cardozo to a rare degree with the qualities that are the special requisites for the work of the Court in whose keeping is entrusted in no small measure the destiny of the nation. That Cardozo should have attained the preeminence that he did after so short a tenure is all the more striking when regard is had to the fact that he sat on the Court during one of the most tempestuous periods in its history.

Cardozo did not derive significance because he was the mouthpiece of the Court in what lawyers call "great cases," though he spoke for the Court in a few of them. It is characteristic of his work that he imparted distinction to whatever he touched, to cases great or small, to cases involving large public issues or turning on narrow technicality. His work in its entirety carried distinction. Thus it is invidious to suggest representative samples of Cardozo's creative legal learning or of his art in opinion-writing. Cardozo's influence survives not because of this or that opinion, but by reason of the underlying philosophy, the attitude of mind, the balanced judgment which infused all of his opinions, of which he wrote some 150 on the Supreme Court.

Any other six might as well be chosen as those to which reference is here made as illustrative of his quality. Of these six, three were essentially the concern of private litigants, three had important public aspects; in three he spoke for the Court, in three he was in dissent. They are: *Reed v. Allen*, 286 U.S. 191, 201 (dissent), because of its resourcefulness in making the law of remedies an instrument of justice; *Stewart Dry Goods Co. v. Lewis*, 294 U.S. 550, 566 (dissent), because of its illuminating analysis of problems of taxation; *McCandless v. Furlaud*, 296 U.S. 140, because it proves that the law of corporate trusteeship can subordinate the skill of individual chicanery; *Ashton v. Cameron County District*, 298 U.S. 513, 632 (dissent), because it demonstrates, with a persuasiveness that eventually carried the day, that the distribution of power between the nation and the states need not entail the impotence of both; the *Social Security Cases*, 301 U.S. 548, and 301 U.S. 619, because of the proof that the Constitution does not preclude the federal system from meeting exigent and pervasive human needs; *Palko v. Connecticut*, 302 U.S. 319, because of its penetrating exposition of the task confronting the Court in applying the Due Process Clause of the Fourteenth Amendment.

A word ought to be said about Cardozo's nonjudicial writings. As a reflective judge, he brooded much on what it is that judges do and how they do it. The fruit of his reflections he expressed in four volumes, slight in size but full of insight drawn from deep learning: *The Nature of the Judicial Process* (1921); *The Growth of the Law* (1924); *Paradoxes of Legal Science* (1928); *Law and Literature* (1931). By deftly spelling out much that was implicit in the early writings of Holmes and trenchantly analyzing what others only gropingly felt, *The Nature of the Judicial Process* has established itself as a little classic. The essay form chosen by Cardozo—suggestive analysis and illumination as against the rigidities of a system in the more or less dogmatic form of a treatise—admirably suited Cardozo's intellectual temper and was well adapted to lay bare the contending and often contradictory claims for which a sensitive and well-balanced process of adjustment affords the best assurance of a just result.

XXIV

Charles Culp Burlingham

On August 31, 1959, Charles Culp Burlingham celebrated his 100th birthday, thus adding one more extraordinary event to an already extraordinary life. Mr. Justice Frankfurter took note of the occasion by a letter to *The New York Times* extolling the qualities of "C. C. B." Too soon thereafter, he had the sadder task of preparing a memorial statement that was published both in the 1960 *Memorial Book of The Association of the Bar of the City of New York* and the *Harvard Law Review* 74:433 (January 1961). It is the latter piece that is reproduced here.

When informed that it was planned to award him the Association's medal for "exceptional contributions to the honor and standing of the bar in this community," C. C. B. advised President Whitney North Seymour that he must decline the honor. "I have done nothing exceptional," he wrote, "and when I evoke the shades of our founders and their successors and recall their contributions, I am confirmed in my conviction that I should not permit myself to be singled out from among my brethren. Though I am not shy, it would embarrass me." Among the shades thus evoked were doubtless Samuel J. Tilden, William M. Evarts, James C. Carter, Joseph H. Choate, and Elihu Root. C. C. B. was conspicuously lacking in exaggerated self-evaluation, singularly devoid of self-deception. Giving the phrase "exceptional contributions" a specific, narrow content, it is not at all surprising that C. C. B. found himself not measuring up to these early giants of the bar. He doubtless felt he lacked their magnitude. In addition to preeminence at the bar, all but Carter attained national and even international distinction in public affairs, and Carter was a scholar in the law. C. C. B. was broadly cultivated but not a scholar; he greatly served his city, state, and nation but never held high office as did, and notably so, Tilden, Evarts, Choate, and Root; accomplished lawyer though he was, both as strategist in important litigation, wise counselor, skillful cross-examiner, he did not make the powerful impact upon the profession and the courts as did those with whom he doubtless compared himself when confronted with President Seymour's proposal.

In thus evoking the shades of "our founders and their successors" and in recalling their contributions, C. C. B. probably saw them through the haze of history which benevolently dims limitations. Even with full allowance for these, C. C. B. was quite right in finding that his efforts and achievements were not like unto the "contributions to the honor and standing of the bar in this community" which were "exceptional" in the case of the great leaders of the bar in C. C. B.'s earlier days, whose memory he so gratefully cherished. But he was quite wrong in applying a merely historical yardstick for determining what contributions are "exceptional," quite wrong in not realizing the uniquity of his own distinction.

C. C. B. had not done anything "exceptional," if any one accomplishment in his life had to be isolated from the totality of it—some conspicuous deed, some notable piece of advocacy, a single act of great statesmanship, a book like James C. Carter's on jurisprudence. His biographer will not be dealing with a sequence of appointments or elections to high public office, the sponsorship of an important measure on the floor of the Senate, a diplomatic triumph, forensic achievement on the national or international scene. Barring only membership on the Board of Education of the City of New York, C. C. B. was all his long life, a wholly private citizen; but as such his influence permeated in vital ways the public life of city, state, and nation.

Charles Culp Burlingham was born in Plainfield, New Jersey, August 31, 1858, the son of the Rev. Dr. Aaron Hale and Emma Starr Burlingham. He entered Harvard, a shy and lonely lad, knowing nobody in Cambridge except another boy who had come from St. Louis, Frank W. Taussig, later to become the famous economist, with whom and his family, including the eminent Dr. Helen Taussig, he became lifelong friends. In 1879 he got his A.B. from Harvard and then moved on to Columbia Law School for his legal education, which gave him its LL.B in 1881. Admitted to the New York bar on September 15 of that year, he began what was probably a uniquely long and rich career at the New York bar. After brief affiliations first with Bangs and Stetson and then with Theron G. Stong, he transferred in 1883 to the office of Wing, Shoudy and Putnam, the firm with which in its various transmutations, he was connected for the rest of his life. He became a member of the firm in 1889; in 1898 the name was changed to Wing, Putnam and Burlingham; in 1899 Cowen, Wing, Putnam and Burlingham. In 1910 Mr. Burlingham became the head of the firm, then called Burlingham, Montgomery and Beecher; in 1918 it became Burlingham, Veeder, Masten and Fearey; in 1928 Burlingham, Veeder, Fearey, Clark and Hupper; in 1934 Burlingham, Veeder, Clark and Hupper. On January 1, 1942, he retired from regular membership and became counsel to the firm, (which on January 1, 1953, became Burlingham, Hupper and Kennedy) remaining so until his death, June 6, 1959.

It was by chance, not by predilection, that C. C. B. became an admiralty specialist, recognized within that close and able fraternity, the admiralty bar, as one of its leaders. Among his partners were some of the most scholarly lawyers of their day. C. C. B. was not self-deprecatory in regarding men like Harrington Putnam, Van Vechten Veeder, Norman B. Beecher, Everett Masten as his professional superiors. But he had other qualities which, together with his ample professional competence, gave him power and distinction beyond what mere professional superiority could command.

And so, while as a technical lawyer, he may not have equalled in learning some of his partners and others at the admiralty bar, in devising the strategy of a large litigation, in knowing the limits of cross-examination, in seizing upon the essentials of a case, in wisely directing the course of an argument, both below and before the Supreme Court, he was second to none. It is an interesting happenstance that C. C. B. argued the first case heard, on October 27, 1891, in the new Circuit Court of Appeals for the Second Circuit. (*The Sarah Cullen*, 48 Fed. 166.) In all his manifestations he had dash—style—conveyed through an agreeable presence, enhanced by a charming voice, clarity and precision of speech, drawing heavily upon a well-stocked memory, particularly of the Bible and Shakespeare. These ingredients, making for persuasiveness, were employed in his arguments before the Supreme Court in a number of important admiralty cases: *The Styria*, 186 U.S. 1; *The Titanic*, 233 U.S. 718; *United States v. Hamburg-American Co.*, 239 U.S. 466; *Standard Oil Co. v. Southern Pacific*, 268 U.S. 146.

Long before Elihu Root summarized the significant role of the lawyer in society by his phrase "the public profession of the law," C. C. B. began to act upon that conception by his energetic efforts in advancing the standards and conduct of bar and bench. The cause nearest to his heart, to which he gave effective devotion throughout his life, was an independent and qualified judiciary. One may say with assurance that no lawyer labored as persistently, as shrewdly and as successfully in getting good men on the courts in New York, both city and state, and on the federal bench throughout the country, as did C. C. B. Of course, he did not do this singlehanded, but the profession and the public is more indebted to C. C. B. than to any other one person for the judicial career of Benjamin N. Cardozo and for bringing to the federal bench Judges Learned and Augustus N. Hand, Charles M. Hough, and Henry G. Ward. One can also be sure, though it cannot be documented, that he was equally effective in preventing unworthy aspirants from obtaining places on the New York state judiciary and the federal bench. His achievement as a maker of judges was partly if not largely due to his intimate relations with the appointing power, especially President Taft and Attorney General Wickersham, and the various governors of New York, irrespective of party affiliations—Al Smith, Franklin Roosevelt, Herbert Lehman, Tom Dewey—with all of whom he carried great weight. This most fruitful aspect of C. C. B.'s life serves as an illustration of Bagehot's emphasis on the importance of influence—wise and honorable persuasiveness—exerted from the outside upon those wielding political power.

Nor was Burlingham indifferent to improvements of the substantive law. In 1909 and again in 1910 he was a member of the American delegation appointed by our Secretary of State at the Brussels Conferences on Maritime Law which dealt with, and drafted international treaties on, collisions and salvage. His interest was equally active in law reform outside his specialty. He was one of the founders of the

American Law Institute, and as a member of its Council his influence was felt in guiding the general direction of the Institute as well as in specific areas of its Restatements.

The international reach of admiralty inevitably brought C. C. B. into professional relations with British lawyers, and his charming companionability led to warm friendship with some of the leading men of the bar and bench across the Atlantic. Among his intimates were John Simon (who, as Viscount Simon, became Lord Chancellor), Robert A. Wright (later as Baron Wright of Durley, Lord of Appeal in Ordinary), Lord Justice McKinnon, and Lord Justice Scrutton. C. C. B. was a man who kept his friendships in repair. Thus, he and Lord Justice McKinnon maintained a steady correspondence for forty years. When McKinnon died, it was characteristic of C. C. B.'s exercise of friendship as well as of his comprehensive interest in law and lawyers throughout the English-speaking world, to make known to our bar, in a letter to *The New York Times* (January 29, 1946), the qualities of that notable English lawyer and judge.

C. C. B.'s zeal for a worthy bench was matched by his zeal for a worthy city. To both causes he gave the resourceful energy of his long life. He was an ardent and proud New Yorker. In him, civic pride aroused civic responsibility. From his early New York days to the very end he associated himself with municipal reform movements. He was concerned not merely for clean government. For him that was only one of the agencies, though the most important, for promoting a civilized community, and civilization presupposed beauty in all its manifestations. By force of his astuteness, rendered effective by a total want of personal ambition, he became the dominant influence in securing for New York the two cleanest and most progressive administrations.

It was C. C. B.'s resourcefulness and will which fused the discordant anti-Tammany forces in making possible the selection and election of John Purroy Mitchell as mayor in 1913 and of Fiorello La Guardia in 1933. Considering the personalities of the Little Flower and C. C. B.—their spontaneity, charm, and wit—it is not at all surprising that the older man, with deeper insight into the ways of the world, could deal with some of the short-sighted outbursts of La Guardia's temperament more effectively than anyone else. He was a staunch and creative ally of Park Commissioner Moses in the beautification of the city and in expanding its amenities. Nor was he merely a worker behind the scenes. With his ready pen he enlisted public opinion through the press for the city's well-being, as for instance in safeguarding ornaments of the city like Washington Square and asserting the authority of the Municipal Art Commission in connection with the Castle Clinton National Monument.

As an enemy of corruption in all its phases, he had no small share in the appointment of Tom Dewey by Governor Lehman as Special Prosecutor of New York County in 1936. After persuading Dewey to accept the nomination for district attorney in the summer of 1937, he was chairman of his campaign committee. While C. C. B. was never a hot political partisan, he was an independent Democrat; and so in 1938 he opposed Dewey as governor "with equal keenness," as he said, and supported Governor Lehman. It is an index to the kind of man C. C. B. was that all this was done with relaxed good humor, so that when Dewey eventually became governor, C. C. B.'s relations and influence with Dewey were unimpaired.

As the lawyer in C. C. B. did not absorb the citizen, the lawyer and citizen did not absorb the whole man. In the range and richness of his interests, in his versatile human relations, and the extent to which it was true that nothing human was alien to him, C. C. B. was something of a Renaissance character. But in C. C. B.'s case it was not true, as too often it is, that ranging over the whole spectrum of life was pretentious shallowness. The nature of the man belied pretentiousness in any form. Life was his flair. He partook of it and added to it, in all his wide encounters. He loved the stage and was on terms of friendship with some of its great notabilities—Edwin Booth, Ellen Terry, Joseph Jefferson, Robert Taylor, Julia Marlowe. He was a hundred years old when he vigorously concerned himself with finding an appropriate biographer for his beloved Ruth Draper. All the arts engaged his interest and all the great artists of our day—painters, sculptors, architects, writers—were among his friends.

His two universities—Harvard and Columbia—profited greatly from his imagination and pertinacity in furthering the true functions of a university. In matters academic he also worked both behind the scenes and spoke out, with his quiet courage, when the occasion called for public utterance. This did not prevent him from being chosen president both of the Harvard University Alumni Association and the Columbia Law School Association, and both universities honored themselves by conferring on him their LL.D.

He was a devoted and broadminded churchman. The son of a Baptist minister, as a student at Harvard College he fell under the influence of Bishop Phillips Brooks and became an Episcopalian. In New York he eventually joined St. George's Church, became a vestryman in 1914, junior warden in 1934, and successor to George W. Wickersham as senior warden in 1936, which he remained to the end. His influence in the Church extended beyond St. George's. He was a delegate to the annual diocesan conventions of the New York diocese from 1920 to 1955, and an unofficial counsellor to more than one Bishop of New York. Characteristically, he was an important promoter of an amendment to New York's Religious Corporations Law to make women eligible as church wardens and vestrymen, and he persisted, until success crowned his efforts, in having the New York diocese change its canons so as to permit the election of women. He lived to see one of them elected.

His great influence with New York newspapers calls for special mention. Reference has already been made to his letters to the press when he deemed it wise to mobilize public opinion or to enlighten it. He wrote on a great variety of subjects—the judiciary; the effective way of countering Tammany; aspects of civil liberties; a plea against the execution of Sacco and Vanzetti; personalities; the role of television. But the letters over his signature tell a small part of his relation to the press. On matters within his range calling for editorial comment, he was a sought adviser and had the welcome ear of a succession of editors of *The New York Times* and *The New York Herald Tribune*.

C. C. B. was Victorian as a letter-writer. In volume and in quality he was one of the great practitioners of that obsolescent art. He had the rare gift of conveying his personality on paper, thereby vastly extending the range and depth of his influence. His letters were sheer delight. They were such a mixture of the *mot juste*, delicate fancy, innocent raillery, tidbits on correct English usage, unmalicious vignettes, all, as often as not, wrapping up a sly reference to the real purpose of the letter, recommending or resisting some measure or judicial appointment. President Franklin Roosevelt was reported to have said that no letters "did he enjoy as much as those from Charlie Burlingham."

This is not the occasion, nor has this writer the deftness of pen and imaginative perception, for attempting an analysis of the persuasive charm of his personality and the qualities of mind and temper by which he exercised his great influence and indubitably made "exceptional contributions to the honor and standing of the bar in this community." (Incidentally, he finally yielded, and in 1953 did accept the Association's Medal.) Lytton Strachey would have found in C. C. B. ample opportunity for the hero-resistant sharpness of his pen and Lord David Cecil would not miss in him elusive qualities less challenging to his subtle probing than those he found in his *Melbourne*. It is safe to say, however, that both Strachey and Cecil would have been captivated by C. C. B.'s charm and disarmed by his unstuffy yet wholly disinterested pursuit of the good and the true. And their well-curbed enthusiasm would have been excited, not by the fact that C. C. B. lived to be nearly 101 years old, but that he reached this venerable age with a mind as lively and voracious as ever, a memory accurate and uncluttered by irrelevant details, its curiosity about men and events undimmed, not concerned with self, conveying his intellectual aliveness with precision and wit.

Mr. Burlingham married Louisa W. Lawrence on September 29, 1883, who died December 7, 1937. There were three children: Charles Burlingham, Dr. Robert Burlingham (who predeceased him), and Miss Nancy Burlingham. A number of grandchildren and numerous great-grandchildren, with all of whom C. C. B. had gay and warm relations, survive him.

He became a member of the Association in December 1882. He served on many of its committees and was our president for two terms, 1929 to 1931. The vivacity of his annual reports and his service as president are too recent to be recalled here.

XXV

Zechariah Chafee, Jr.

This memorial essay on Professor Chafee was first published in the 1960 *Yearbook of the American Philosophical Society* (pp. 126–31) and the *Harvard Law Review* 74:440 (January 1961).

ZECHARIAH CHAFEE, JR., left a record of enduring distinction in the triune phase of a law professor's creative opportunities: he was an inspiring teacher, he was a fruitful scholar, he was a skillful draftsman of an important measure of law reform. In these accomplishments his eminence was not unique. But the extent to which through his scholarship he influenced the thought and temper of public opinion and action in that pervasive aspect of national life known as civil rights has no match in the legal professoriate.

Zechariah Chafee, Jr., was born in Providence, Rhode Island, December 7, 1885, of Yankee stock, the son of Zechariah and Mary Dexter (Sharpe) Chafee. His father was an iron founder in Providence, his mother was a descendant of Roger Williams. Chafee was educated at Brown University, with which his family had long been associated, and from which he graduated in 1907. After three years' trial in his father's iron foundry, convinced that industry was not for him, he entered the Harvard Law School in 1910. There he confirmed his natural proclivity for the law. Upon graduating with distinction in 1913, he returned to Providence to practice law. Three years of that convinced him that scholarship, not the immediate practicalities of life, was indicated for him, and in the fall of 1916 he accepted a call to the Harvard Law School faculty.

For forty years, until the end, his work at Harvard was the center of his life. From it radiated his extraordinary personal influence as a teacher, issued his contributions to learning, impressive both in quality and volume, and, *ex cathedra*, he served as draftsman and counselor of legislation. These accomplishments would have combined to make Chafee a memorable figure in the history of American law-teaching and law. An even more notable place in the history of American legal scholarship is bound to be his because national leadership came to him, as a scholar, unsought but indisputable, in the cause of freedom of speech as basic to the pursuit of the American dream.

Joining a law faculty of eminence, including some of his own former teachers, Chafee quickly made his own place. He was equally exhilarating in dealing with one of the dreariest branches of the law—negotiable instruments—as he was in the more exciting field of equity. The range and subtlety of problems of equitable jurisdiction were especially congenial to the flexibility and adventuresomeness of Chafee's mind as it was appropriate for his wide culture and the diversity of his learning outside the law. See *Cases on Equitable Remedies; Cases on Equity; Some Problems of Equity: Five Lectures Delivered at the University of Michigan, 1949.* To a degree unusual in modern scholars, he was an acknowledged master in the areas of the law that were his specialized concern and competently roamed far and wide outside the law. His culture had depth derived not only from the wide field of English literature. He was at home in the classics and read them for pleasure; he was also a mathematician of no mean scope. And so he was not confined within the narrow grooves of his immediate specialties.

Like all inspiring teachers, Chafee saw interdependencies in the realm of the mind. He brought illumination on so-called technical legal problems from related fields, if not of knowledge, at least from relevant processes for obtaining understanding. Generations upon generations of men left the Harvard Law School aroused in their capacity for thinking, excited by the adventures of the mind, widened in their horizons, because they had been students of Zechariah Chafee. They carried the impress of his influence in their future work as lawyers, judges, administrators, legislators, and, not least, as future teachers of law. In 1919 he became a full professor of law; in 1938 he was given the famed Langdell chair in the Law School; and in 1950, in recognition of a scholarship that cut across several of the faculties, Harvard conferred upon Chafee the rare honor of making him a University Professor. As such he continued teaching in the Law School but was also enabled to give competent undergraduates the benefit of the ferment he was capable of imparting in a course entitled "Fundamental Human Rights."

As is true of so much of our law, our federal system begets difficult problems which do not bother the home of our law, England. The problem of effectively settling multiple claims against a single individual is vastly complicated in this country when claims originate in several states. The solution of the problem required legislation. With great skill Chafee drafted the enactment which became the Federal Interpleader Act of 1936. Long after he had attained a national reputation in a far wider and more important field, Chafee regarded this piece of legislation as his principal professional accomplishment.

But it was his immersion in problems of equity that led to much more far-reaching use of his powers than drafting and securing the enactment of the Federal Interpleader Act, and assured Chafee's permanent place in American history, for such it will be, as leader in the maintenance and advance of the spirit of liberty in the United States. But unlike perhaps all other great promoters of this cause, Chafee was not an instinctive reformer or evangelist. Just as Darwin submitted his findings on the origin of species not as a heretic but as a naturalist, so Chafee became the outstanding expounder of freedom of speech, both within the protection of the Constitution and as a matter of policy, not as a crusader but as a scholar. The impulse to this undesigned and unexpected transmutation of a quiet scholar into one of the most controversial university figures and, gradually, one of the most powerful influences in promoting the moral health of the nation can best be stated by quoting Professors Mark Howe and Archibald MacLeish, in their joint minute on behalf of the Faculty of the Law School and the Faculty of Arts and Sciences of Harvard University:

> It was his [Chafee's] own opinion, given on numerous occasions, that he had backed into controversy quite by accident in the course of his speculations on Equity's power to enjoin libel, since such speculations involve a man sooner or later in consideration of the Constitutional guarantees of freedom of speech and expression.

However, as they went on to say, the interest thus aroused in Chafee was intensified by an article in support of Mr. Justice Holmes' famous dissent in *Abrams v. United States*, 250 U.S. 616, a prosecution under the Espionage Act of the First World War which resulted in what were widely deemed to be brutal sentences. (A Contemporary State Trial—*United States v. Abrams*, Harv. L. Rev. 33:747.) This article led to accusations against the rectitude of Chafee's scholarship which were heard and dismissed by a Committee To Visit the Harvard Law School, consisting of some of the most distinguished judges in the land. This experience undoubtedly energized the temperamentally easy-going Chafee into persistence in the cause of promoting what to him were ancient liberties, and exposing the unworthiness, both as a matter of law and as a matter of national tradition, of postwar tendencies toward repression. He had already published, in 1920, his *Freedom of Speech.* Professors Howe and MacLeish were, I believe, right in stating that because of the *Abrams* case incident this book became "the master directive of Chafee's life." This book was in itself a landmark in the literature on the subject. It became the arsenal of resistance to measures both legislative and executive and thereby served as a curb to what would have been much more indefensible legislation and repressive conduct.

Chafee's weapons were always those of the scholar, whether in speech or in writing. As a scholar he continued his studies in the field of his book and the result, in 1941, was his *Free Speech in the United States.* This is not only a revision of the earlier book but a rethinking and a rewriting of it, with a detachment and intellectual scrupulosity as though he were dealing with a technical legal subject uninvolved in public emotion. He gave comfort neither to politicians exploiting fear nor to doctrinaires who find in the Constitution compulsions of literalness, unmindful of its history and of John Marshall's guiding principle that "it is a *constitution* we are expounding." In his writings, books, articles, pamphlets, letters to the press, as in his utterances, speeches, formal addresses, testimony before legislative committees, he conveyed his strong convictions with persuasive gentleness. For his dominant strain was compassion, a fellow-feeling for his kind, not, as too often mars reformers, hate of those who opposed or obstructed his vision. In his long contest, for such it became, with political and obscurantist forces, he did not turn into a partisan propagandist; he relied on the leverage of scholarship to recall the nation to what he believed to be its history and tradition. These he expounded in a succession of notable books of scholarship: *Documents on Fundamental and Human Rights; How Human Rights Got Into the Constitution; Government and Mass Communications; Three Human Rights in the Constitutions of 1787.* Nor did he allow his focus to be narrowed and his perspective to be warped by shutting out other interests. He was an essayist of charm and urbanity, as revealed in his volume *The Inquiring Mind.* Like all deep students of the law, he found himself delving into legal history, as manifested in an important paper on "Colonial Courts And The Common Law" and the "Early Records of the Rhode Island Court of Equity." The quality of his scholarship and the reach of his interests are well illustrated in three papers in the *Proceedings* of our Society, a member of which he was elected in 1946: "Do Judges Make or Discover Law" (*Proc. Amer. Philos. Soc.* 91:405); "Charles Evans Hughes" (*ibid.* 93:267); "Some Problems of the Draft International Conventions on Human Rights" (*ibid.* 95:471).

While he never held public office, he responded to calls for public service. Thus he was one of the *amici curiae* appointed by U.S. Circuit Judge George W. Anderson in cases arising out of the challenged misconduct of the Department of Justice in the first World War. See *Colyer v. Skeffington*, 265 Fed. 17. He was a member of the important Committee on the Bill of Rights of the American Bar Association and had a major share in the brief submitted by that committee in the leading case of *Hague v. CIO*, 307 U.S. 496, 678. He was a member of the Commission on Freedom of the Press, a member of the United Nations Subcommittee on Freedom of Information and the Press, and a member of the United States delegation to United

Nations conference at Geneva which formulated the Covenant on Human Rights.

Chafee married Bess Frank Searle July 20, 1912. Of the marriage were four children, Zechariah III, Robert S. (who predeceased him), Annie C., and Ellen C. He died in Cambridge on February 8, 1957, following a recurring heart attack, not long after expounding the fruits of his lifelong scholarship on "Fundamental Human Rights" to a wide audience reached in his Lowell television lectures. In him American legal scholarship and the worldwide fellowship of the free spirit of man lost one of the sweetest, most fruitful, and valiant of its contributors.

XXVI

Monte M. Lemann

There are a few great lawyers in each generation whose greatness is revealed primarily through the practice of law and leadership of the legal community unconnected with public office. Monte M. Lemann was one of these. This memorial piece by his good friend Mr. Justice Frankfurter was first published in the 1960 *Memorial Book of the Association of the Bar of the City of New York* and the *Harvard Law Review* 74:445 (January 1961).

FROM A rare occasion a tired cliché can gain fresh vitality. And so, one may unashamedly dare to say that Monte Lemann was an ornament of his profession—for he was that. In the changing circumstances under which law is practiced in our day, particularly the diminishing significance of spectacular forensic exhibitions, national recognition even within the profession comes to few lawyers. It did to Monte Lemann. This is all the more remarkable since his virtues were unostentatious, his considerable endowments modestly applied, his strong will gently exerted. His thorough and lifelong professional training, joined to practical sagacity, made him a much sought counselor of large and varied interests; his scholarly bent enabled him to be an effective force in the life of the two universities of his allegiance, Tulane and Harvard; his grasp of the functions of history, theory, and the felt needs of the time in shaping law weightily contributed to the work of the American Law Institute; his instinctive straightforwardness saved him from subordinating clear understanding to the claims of short-sighted expediency, when he had to deal, as a member of the Wickersham Commission, with the grave moral and political problems raised by the Eighteenth Amendment.

Monte Lemann (his full name was Montefiore Mordecai Lemann) was born on April 3, 1884, at Donaldsonville, Louisiana, the son of Jewish parents, Bernard and Harriet Freidheim Lemann. His forebears had been settled in Louisiana for generations. After the preliminary public school education, he received the Bachelor of Arts degree from Tulane in 1902 and from Harvard in 1903. He proceeded to the Harvard Law School, where he graduated with honors in 1906, continuing his theoretical legal education as a member of the Tulane Law Faculty from 1909 until his appointment to the Wickersham Commission (National Commission on Law Observance and Enforcement) in 1929. Duly admitted to the Louisiana bar, he began practice in New Orleans with the firm of Saunders & Gurley, successor to White & Saunders, of which Edward Douglass White, the future Chief Justice of the United States, had been a member. Upon the appointment of Mr. Saunders to the United States District Court and the death of Hughes Gurley, the practice of the firm and its associates was taken over by the firm of Hall & Monroe, composed of Harry H. Hall and J. Blanc Monroe. Lemann became a partner in 1909, when its name was changed to Hall, Monroe & Lemann. This it remained, following Hall's death in 1911, until the retirement of Chief Justice Frank Adair Monroe (father of J. Blanc Monroe) from the Supreme Court of Louisiana in 1922 and his association with this firm as counsel, at which time the name Monroe & Lemann was adopted. Lemann remained its active member until his death September 13, 1959, happily joined in recent years by his two sons, Thomas B. and Stephen B.

Monte Lemann was an all-around lawyer with an extensive practice. Only patents and criminal law were outside its range. He was equally effective in counseling a variety of clients engaged in diverse enterprises, local and farflung, as a trial lawyer, and before the Supreme Court of the United States, even as he proved himself a notable government lawyer when he served as assistant chief counsel of the United States Shipping Board during the first World War.

Among the busiest of lawyers, his conscience enabled him to generate the necessary energy to be able to pay the debt which, we have been admonished, every lawyer owes to his profession. Several agencies for needed law reform drew on his copious talents and wide experience. In addition to his significant role as a member of the Council of the American Law Institute, he was one of the moving spirits of the Louisiana State Law Institute, a powerful engine for modernizing particularly the procedural law of that state. Legal aid was a special concern of his. He fathered it in his part of the country and was a director of both the New Orleans and the National Legal Aid Societies.

His qualities and capacities and services were gratifyingly recognized by bar and bench. He was president of both the New Orleans Bar Association and the Louisiana State Bar Association; the National Legal Aid Society gave him the Reginald Heber Smith Award for service to legal aid. He was an obvious selection as a member of the strong Supreme Court's Advisory Committee on the Rules of Civil Procedure, under the chairmanship of former Attorney General William D. Mitchell, and as such he did yeoman service from its inception on June 3, 1935 (295 U.S. 774) to its discharge on October 1, 1956. (U.S. Supreme Court Journal, 1956, p. 3.)

Twice the Supreme Court, *tempore* Hughes, C. J., utilized him as Special Master in complicated and important controversies between states: *Arkansas v. Tennessee*, 301 U.S. 666; 310 U.S. 563, and the *Illinois Waterways* case, 309 U.S. 569, 636; 311 U.S. 107; 313 U.S. 547. In both cases Master Lemann's findings and conclusions were in all respects confirmed by the Court.

His combination of learning, balanced judgment, convictions with tolerance, a strong sense of fair play, power of comprehensive analysis and capacity for dispatching business, admirably equipped him to be a judge. When President Roosevelt offered him a seat on the Court of Appeals for the Fifth Circuit, personal circumstances precluded acceptance.

Though law in all its aspects and attractions was the mainstay of his life, the lawyer in him did not absorb the citizen. He served his city, state, region, and nation in their educational, charitable and social endeavors. In his quietly effective way, as trustee of Dillard University, a local Negro institution, he promoted healthier race relations, long before its issues were dramatized, through the key medium of education. It was characteristic of him that he, the youngest and in his own mind the least important of the eleven members of the Wickersham Commission, did not flinch from the courage of his wisdom that there was "no alternative but repeal of the Eighteenth Amendment." 1 Rep. Natl. Commn. on Law Observance and Enforcement 139, 148. (January 7, 1931.) It was characteristic of him that his greatest reluctance in avowing this conclusion was his sense of modesty in dissociating himself from the contrary view of his ten associates.

Indeed, when one contemplates the self-deprecatory qualities of Monte Lemann and the extent to which clients, his brethren at the bar, courts from the lowest to the highest, institutions, both governmental and private, promoters of causes indispensable to the country's well-being, sought his counsel, relied on his guidance and drew on his strength, Monte Lemann becomes comfortingly striking proof of Emerson's homely wisdom that men somehow or other find their way to the maker of the best mouse-trap.

On December 7, 1921, Monte Lemann married Nettie E. Hyman, the mother of his two sons. After an extraordinarily gallant, almost gay, fight against the ravages of tuberculosis before the present curative procedures were available, she died in July 1946. On October 11, 1947, he married Mildred C. Lyons, who survives him.

Monte Lemann became an associate member of our Association on March 11, 1934. He was a member of the Special Committee on the Federal Loyalty-Security Program which rendered the report that received nation-wide attention. (Report of the Special Committee on The Federal Loyalty-Security Program of The Association of the Bar of the City of New York, Dodd, Mead & Company, New York, 1956.)

XXVII

Edmund M. Morgan

As Mr. Justice Frankfurter notes in this essay, Professor Edmund M. Morgan ranks with James Bradley Thayer and John Henry Wigmore as America's greatest students of the law of evidence. He was a longtime friend and colleague of Mr. Justice Frankfurter during his tenure at Yale, Harvard, and Vanderbilt law schools. When, in 1961, the law review of Vanderbilt University undertook to produce an issue honoring Professor Morgan, the Justice was naturally called upon to express his appreciation of the man and the scholar (14:706, June 1961).

THE ROMAN admonition *de mortuis nil nisi bonum* bespeaks generosity of spirit because it implies, at least in part, that since of some people the truth could not be told during their lives, they should not be pursued after they are gone. Happily, of Eddie Morgan, even his "warts"—with all his tenacious loyalties, he would disown a friend who claimed perfection for him—are endearing or, at least, his limitations emphasize his great qualities. It is an easy and gladsome task to report him aright, and so I rejoice that the *Vanderbilt Law Review* has decided to tell him to his face what is thought of him. Thousands of lawyers scattered all over the land, hundreds of law teachers, judges on every bench, trial and appellate, are, if they know their craft, consciously indebted to him and many more are his debtors without awareness of their obligation. And beyond his services to the functionaries of the law, he has been, and fortunately continues to be, a significant contributor to the very process of law. To speak of this not merely adequately but at all I must leave to others. Even were I not barred by lack of special competence within the areas of his preoccupying labors, a due estimate of what difference Morgan's teaching and writing have made to the law would require time not at my disposal. But I would not miss the chance to utter a word of affection for Eddie Morgan as a lifelong friend, and admiration for him both as a scholar and as an exemplar for the legal profession in all its phases.

As friend and student of the law, I have, of course, followed his writings, though to be sure not systematically. With a view to refreshing my recollection of its corpus, not, as I have indicated, to descant upon it but by way of recalling the man, I asked those admirable coworkers, the staff of the Supreme Court Library, to bring together all of Professor Morgan's publications. I knew that he was rather scribacious, but I hardly expected to be staggered by the sizable Morgan library with which I was confronted. On a rough estimate, there were some two hundred items of every variety of legal writing: text books, case books, an unpretentious but wise little volume on the *Introduction to the Study of Law,* the successive stages of the Code of Evidence of the American Law Institute, essays scattered in dozens of law reviews, as well as those contained between book covers, like his Carpentier Lectures, book reviews, surveys of developments in the law both in the nation and latterly in Tennessee. He has not been a one-subject scholar. But in one field, Evidence, he has become the contemporary master. History will surely account him with Thayer and Wigmore as a trinity in the law of evidence, and not the less so because of his respectful but fresh reexamination of and disagreement with some of the tenets of his two glorious predecessors. Nor has he restricted his great powers to doctrinal writings. If law is indeed to serve as the cohesive force of a civilized secular society, Morgan naturally has not shrunk from applying his deep learning in the fields of evidence and procedure—that is, the appropriate conduct of trials—to such *cause celebres* as the Mooney and Sacco-Vanzetti cases, even though or precisely because, they were embroiled in public passion.

Needless to say, I did not read this vast body of Morgan literature, but I did scurry through enough of it to renew my sense of his range, depth, subtle powers of analysis, horse-sense, a scholar's twin faculties of intellectual courage and modesty. He has also been heedful of Mr. Justice Holmes' hint to judges that in order to be weighty they need not be heavy. I cannot resist the temptation to quote *in toto* the way in which Morgan disposed of an unworthy book: "If false, a most outrageous libel upon the dead; if true, the biography of an able, attractive, but thoroughly contemptible shyster; in either case an entirely unjustifiable waste of good, white paper."

These summary comments of mine on the characteristics of his writing are in effect a delineation of the man. But it may come as a great surprise to all who love Eddie Morgan to have me say that in my first encounter with him he appeared not unlike an ogre. This occurred when I was a frightened new second-year editor of the *Harvard Law Review* and Morgan was not only a towering third-year man but the Note Editor of that *Review*, exercising powerful blue-penciling authority over my earliest efforts at legal writing. I soon realized that Morgan was not dealing with me as a person, properly making my sensibilities irrelevant. He was dealing with my product, dealing with it as mercilessly as intellectual product should be dealt with. It did not take me long to discover that Morgan, unlike too many people, was not confounding his duty as a critic with generosity of feeling as a friend. That is a rare enough quality in men. Morgan strikingly illustrates a still rarer quality. As he would not make the confusion between intellectual and personal issues where others were involved, he does not think there should be such a confusion of functions where his interest is involved. Many years later, after we had become fast friends—he was at Yale and I at Harvard—the Harvard Law School faculty invited Morgan to join it. For reasons that are here irrelevant as is their soundness, I opposed the call on the ground that the needs of the Harvard Law Faculty at the time were for a reinforcement different from the interests and qualities that Morgan would bring. I wrote him of my views, adding that while I had to vote against calling him no one would more eagerly welcome him to Cambridge than I. How many men would not have deemed such conduct on the part of a friend at least quixotic, if not indeed negativing friendship. Not so Eddie Morgan. He respected my action on the basis of my thinking. Not only was there no bruise to our friendship; the incident deepened it.

Need I say more to convey my affection and my admiration for Eddie Morgan.

XXVIII

Harold Laski

It is not clear whether it was Harold Laski's prodigiousness, his energy, his sparkling and prolific pen, his deep interest in the young, or the other traits which they shared in common that drew Mr. Justice Frankfurter to the younger man. But from 1916 until Laski's death in 1950 there was a deep and abiding affection that each had for the other, an affection that overcame the weaknesses which each thought he saw in the ideals and methods that the other espoused. When, in 1961, the British Broadcasting Company put its "Harold Laski Programme" on the air, it was natural for them to ask Mr. Justice Frankfurter's participation and no less natural for him to respond in the manner that he did.

I AM GRATEFUL to the BBC for inviting me to this symposium and not, of course, because Harold Laski was a friend of mine but because he was a great teacher, and the memory of a great teacher should be kept green.

I visited Canada in the winter of 1915–1916, and, while there, recalled that a friend of mine, Norman Hapgood, who was President Wilson's Ambassador to Denmark, told me of an extraordinary young man he had met at McGill University. Indeed, he was so fired by his experience that he thought I ought to take the next train and see this lad, he, Hapgood, knowing my interest in promising young men. I ought to say I was a professor of law at Harvard University at the time and, naturally, therefore, interested in youth. Thus encouraged, or, rather, almost persuasively

Reprinted with the kind permission of the British Broadcasting Corporation.

coerced, by Ambassador Hapgood, I made for McGill University where this phenomenon called Harold Laski was then a young instructor. Everything that Hapgood said about his extraordinary qualities was verified within an hour. I was charmed by his manner. His quickness, his eagerness, his liveliness, his range of interests—all wholly apart from the learning I was told he possessed—made me realize I was in the presence of a very unusual person. I spent next day with him, and we talked about things of common interest. Since my specialty was public law, which means the relation of the individual to society, and his was political theory, we quickly reached common ground, though we also quickly reached divergence of views. That was a very striking thing from the outset of my acquaintance with him—that he wasn't interested in agreement, that he *was* interested in the exchange of ideas.

When I came back to Cambridge, I saw the then Dean of the Graduate School of Harvard, Charles Haskins, a very distinguished medieval historian, well-known on both sides of the Atlantic. I told him of Laski and the qualities that I was sure I had rightly discerned in him and thought that he was such an extraordinary fellow that Haskins ought to look into him and see if he wasn't a desirable acquisition for Harvard. Haskins became interested, made inquiries, and the short of it is that he soon invited him down to Harvard to become a tutor. He became a tutor in whatever the technical department was called dealing with questions of political science, broadly speaking, government.

And so he came to Cambridge. He was already married and had a child. The details that I found about his past naturally made him even more interesting—that he had married when he was 18; that he graduated as we say in this country—he came down from New College—with high honors. He sought to enlist in the army but was rejected and got a job overseas at McGill, where he was spoken of in the highest terms by all the senior men with whom I talked about him. Almost overnight he became a sensation at Harvard. He had infectious enthusiasm. He excited men with interest in abstract political theories who had been quite immune to such excitation before they came within reach of his influence. For instance, there was a book shop in Cambridge at that time, known as Dunster House, owned by a fellow of independent means who went into the book-shop business as a luxury because he cared about books. Laski had a strong feeling that if a man really cares about books, he must own a book—he must be the possessor of the richness that is contained between the covers of books. And, to an extent unparalleled I think certainly in my lifetime, the Dunster book shop became a prosperous, commercial enterprise because Laski affected his students, indeed infected them, so that they bought books. On the whole, most American college students don't buy books. They may buy everything else, but people are chary about buying books, for reasons that I have never been able to understand. And soon that book store was humming, as it were, as an annex to Harvard University. It became, as indeed a good book shop is, not only a club but also an intellectual agency.

I happened to have been a friend of Mr. Justice Holmes, who, in the world of jurisprudence, in the history of law —what shall I say—in juristic mountain ranges would be Mount Everest, and I told Justice Holmes about this wonderful lad. Soon I brought him to see the Justice and they fell to, as is proved by the two wonderful volumes of letters that passed between Mr. Justice Holmes and Laski between 1916 and until within a fortnight of the Justice's death in 1935. That he should have evoked this close intimacy with Justice Holmes—so different in antecedents and more than half a century apart in years—affords striking proof of Laski's extraordinary qualities of mind and heart.

The influence of Laski as a teacher was a permeating influence. Every great teacher not only teaches his students but also teaches his colleagues. He was young. Twenty-three and twenty-four is pretty young for achieving a significant position in the life of so great an institution—great in both senses of the term—as Harvard. When he died there were testimonials about him, of him, by some of the leading scholars at Harvard. To mention two—Charles H. McIlwaine, a great scholar, still alive—he's past ninety now—said that he probably learned more from Laski than any colleague he ever had; and Professor Zechariah Chafee, also well-known on both sides of the ocean, himself an author of great repute in the domain of politics and law. He said he had very few friends with whom he disagreed as much as he did with Harold Laski, but still fewer friends from whom he learned so much as he did from Laski. Well, I could pile on these testimonials.

His influence on men wasn't merely on men who were going to go into the law or destined to become teachers in the field of government, political science, that is, fields kindred to his own interests. He affected everybody who was open to the influence of an exciting, evocative teacher. Students who became architects, manufacturers, business executives, doctors, dentists, writers, playwrights, what not, came under the sway of this young lad. He was a stripling not only in years but in size. I don't believe he weighed 100 pounds; I may be wrong about that. But he was a stripling in every way with an unremitting fluency of speech and a great debater. He loved interchange. He had also what someone rightly called a passionate interest in the young. I think that is almost the key to his significance as a teacher.

He left this country in 1920 to succeed Professor Graham Wallas at the London School of Economics where he remained until his premature death in 1950, but he kept in constant communication with this country both by correspondence and by visiting—I think he came to the States, if not every year, every other year—lectured widely in our universities, was eagerly sought at forums.

This isn't the occasion and certainly I am not the person to talk about the enduring contributions of the man to thought in the fields with which he was preoccupied and which led him into politics. His driving passions were his desire for liberty and his desire to study the conditions under which liberty is best promoted for the mass of mankind. He was a great egalitarian—a good deal of an intellectual snob—but in human relations he was an egalitarian. He got on with anybody and everybody. He started in life, as a matter of fact, as a geneticist and he was sixteen years old when he wrote an article—I forget where—which came to the attention of the founder of genetic science, Sir Francis Galton, who wrote to the magazine, or wherever it appeared, to find out who the author was. He was astounded when he found that the author was a lad, namely, Harold J. Laski, sixteen years old. Galton wrote him a letter in which he said that if he would only stick to genetics he had a great career ahead of him. He didn't stick to genetics. He got interested in politics and was greatly influenced by Sir Ernest Barker, then his tutor at New College.

I suppose I can't be very wrong if I say that the judgment on men by others derives from the point of contact with the men on whom you pass judgment. Now Laski was not an ivory tower scholar. If he had confined himself, for instance, to what was his chief intellectual interest—the political ideas of the sixteenth and seventeenth centuries—he would have gone down in the records of scholarship as a very great scholar in those domains. If he had decided to specialize as an historian, I have no particle of doubt that he would have been one of the distinguished historians dealing with the French Revolution—the period before, during, and after. But politics on its theoretical side was his great intellectual interest. If he had confined himself to that and just written books and articles dealing with the theory of politics—sovereignty, that awful word, sovereignty—and had written heavy books which relatively few people would have read outside of academic institutions, he would have been known in the craft, in the cult, as a notable person. But he didn't confine himself to that.

He had a passionate interest in life and he was also a glib writer and a glib talker, interested not merely in the theory of politics as an end in itself as a scholastic undertaking, but politics as the instrument of begetting a more decent, a more gracious, a more satisfying society, particularly for the underdog. He was very sensitive to the underdog and the underdog everywhere, not merely in England or the United States, but everywhere—India, Africa, etc., etc. And so those who encountered, either directly or through the printed page, Laski on the hustings, would bring to bear their biases in relation to his biases, because he was either promoting or opposing their own notion of how heaven was to be reached on earth, more particularly through the Labor party. He also had a facile, easy pen. He was a journalist, and anyone who read his journalistic performances naturally judged him by the standards with which we judge journalism. He was an extraordinarily facile fellow, not merely the things that he wrote for the daily papers—for the *Daily Herald* or *The Manchester Guardian* or what not—but even heavier articles in learned publications. I remember being with him while he was writing an article for *Foreign Affairs*, Hamilton Fish Armstrong's very solid quarterly, and he wrote a solid article as fast as his fountain pen could move across the page.

The only judgment on a teacher is whether he lives in the minds of his students. Laski was a teacher from 1914 to 1950—thirty-six years—and, he not only seeded his views or his predilections or his preferences into the minds of thousands upon thousands of students all over the world, but he seeded a certain passion for the adventure of the mind. He seeded a certain habit of reading books that are first rate instead of reading *about* books. He seeded excitement in the world of the mind and spirit as few teachers of our time.

And, so, I conclude—and one cannot repeat it too often—that he was a very great teacher, not just a good teacher, but, I think, a very great teacher. It is important to emphasize this because, in all our talk about education, all the pressures for more money and for more buildings and for more this and for more that, education will be barren, education means nothing, unless you have a sufficient number of teachers like Laski. They can't be made. Money can't make them. But they can be encouraged, and the example which they set can serve as a standard for judging the performances of other people.

And, therefore, it is to me a grateful opportunity to pay tribute to Harold Laski, not as a person to whom I was deeply devoted, not as a person who stimulated my own mind, not as a person who made me think about my own profession more effectively than I would have thought without him, but to pay tribute to him as one of the great achievers in that function of man in society which is second to none, namely, the function of a teacher.

XXIX

Learned Hand

On the death of Learned Hand, Mr. Justice Frankfurter contributed two *in memoriam* pieces to publications of the Harvard Law School, an institution in which both men took the greatest pride. The first appeared in the *Harvard Law Review* 75:1 (November 1961); the second in the *1962 Harvard Law School Yearbook* as a dedication of that volume. There is some repetition of ideas in these two pieces on "B. Hand," as the Justice called him, but none that requires apology.

One echoes the few comprehensive words of Mr. Justice Brandeis when news was brought him of his brother Holmes' death: "And so the great man is gone." Not much more can be said about Judge Hand without being redundant.

It is natural to link Learned Hand with Oliver Wendell Holmes. The Judge would not have one claim him to be the seminal thinker the Justice was. The latter powerfully changed the direction of legal thought, first through *The Common Law* (1881) and then from the bench, both of Massachusetts and the Supreme Court. But while Judge Hand was an epigone—he, like Cardozo, reverently called Mr. Justice Holmes "the Master"—he was a master in his own right. Equipped scholarship will in good time assay Learned Hand's significance, and not only in the history of the federal judiciary. Even so restricted, much more is demanded than a critical interpretation of his vast output of opinions, probably nearer three thousand than two. It requires an imaginative, Maitlandlike use of the twenty-five small folio volumes of his handwritten extensive minute-books as District Judge to put these proceedings in the context of the teeming commercial and sociopolitical life of New York City, indeed of the country, during the period (1909–1924). For an account of his long years on the Court of Appeals for the Second Circuit the scholar is to be envied who will have at his disposal for vividly conveying the impressive, joyous labors of that court's unrivaled trinity—Learned Hand, Thomas W. Swan, and Augustus N. Hand—the memoranda they exchanged in every case preliminary to conference and adjudication. Enough is known to make it safe to assume that what "L. H." wrote was in the spirit of Elizabethan and Restoration literature rather than in the more sober style of his formal, public allocutions.

His jurisdiction was confined within the Acts of Congress and the controlling precedents of his hierarchical superiors, but not his authority. His influence radiated to all the courts of the land and thereby improved the corpus and spirit of American law. Suffice it here to say that by his opinions and his dominant role in shaping the various Restatements of the American Law Institute he magisterially affected doctrine in areas of the law lying wholly outside the scope of federal jurisprudence. More than a half century on the bench afforded his insights propitious opportunity to function as a fruitful teacher of law, for education depends not a little on reiteration. Judge Hand liberated bar and bench, perhaps not less pervasively than Holmes and Cardozo, from the bondage of jejune categories and question-begging formulas and thereby enabled them effectively to appreciate that the complexities of life cannot be ruled by unreal simplicities of law.

Of Learned Hand it can surely be said that the style was the man. His writing, whether in his opinion, his public addresses or his letters (and in nothing did he reveal himself more than in his letters), was muscular and ruminative and eloquent, showing traces at times of two of his assertive teachers of philosophy, more of Josiah Royce's less than pellucid subtleties than of the elegance of George Santayana. What of the man? How convey him to those who were denied in not having known him one of the enduring experiences of life? This feeble pen will certainly not attempt to do so. The Judge himself gave us the hint for becoming seized of his personality. He recalled the value that Carlyle attached "to a single picture of a man" compared with books that might be written of him. Learned Hand was fortunate in the "Gardner Cox pixit." There he is: massive and sensitive, reflective and gay, viewing the human situation dubiously and compassionately, at once concentrated and relaxed, ready to listen respectfully to Hume and to joust with Voltaire. And the whole man is there. The painter did not shrink the man in a gown. One is allowed to guess that he was half puritan and half pagan and that Pan was a remote ancestor.

But even the most gifted artist is enabled to convey his subject only through the imaginative eye of the observer. Canvas cannot talk and Learned Hand was a fabulous talker. He was not a coercive monologist, one of those torrential talkers who overwhelm their listeners. He subjugated by delighting. Through his humor and fancy and range he became the center and circumference of every party. This rich talk now remains only treasured memory, but samples of the inimitable raconteur and of his mimic and histrionic gifts will, happily, not float down the stream of history merely on oral tradition. Records, however inadequate, have preserved his unforgettable recital of an episode at a rally in the 1900 Bryan campaign. It concerns the individually contrived use by the various speakers of Oliver Goldsmith's familiar lines

> Ill fares the land, to hast'ning ills a prey,
> Where wealth accumulates, and men decay;

recounted by the Judge in their successive dialects, Plattdeutsch, Yiddish, Down-neck (Newark) Irish, and finally in the golden voice of the Boy Orator of the Platte himself, after an imitation of the latter's oratorical resume of the providentially guided history of this country which the mimic freshly improvised for each occasion. Unless I'm mistaken (I hope I am) the Judge's hilarious repertoire of Gilbert and Sullivan is lost to posterity, but his rendering of some of the less well-known American folksongs is preserved.

However full-throated one's appreciation of him, reference must be made to the fact that Judge Hand did not become Mr. Justice Hand. Of course he should have been on the Supreme Court. Holmes wanted him there while he was still District Judge. He would have met the spacious requirements for a seat on the Supreme Bench as very few men in his time. In addition to his other preeminent qualities, he would have added to literature as well as to the literature of the law by his opinions in the *United States Reports*. Not a little nonsense on why he was not named has been written by those who are ignorant of the fortuitous elements that determine Supreme Court choices. But for Czolgosz's pistol, Mr. Justice Gray's successor would have been not Oliver Wendell Holmes but Alfred Hemenway, a respectable Boston lawyer, whose chief recommendation was his law partnership with President McKinley's Secretary of the Navy. L. Hand was not denied a place on the Court for any specific disqualifying reason—geography or partisan politics or judicial outlook—until, when he was past seventy, age was deemed a bar. Events cast a sardonic smile on this misjudgment, for Judge Hand continued his distinguished judicial labors for more than a decade after the short tenure of the much younger man who was preferred to him.

To bemoan that the turn of the wheel did not put him on the Supreme Court grossly underestimates what he accomplished off it. His opinions for that Court would, of course, carry weight they do not now have. What appears from him in the *Federal Reporter* and the *Federal Supplement* will not on that account lose its durability. It is extremely doubtful whether on the Supreme Court, with its confined area of litigation, he would have influenced the course of law in its widest reaches as much as he did from the Second Circuit and through the Law Institute. In this regard and others, he would have found himself much more circumscribed on the Supreme Court than where he was. Above all, the country would thereby have lost the impact of one of the few free-spirited voices possessed of arresting eloquence, and therefore heeded, to counter fears aroused by timidity and demagogic patriotism with the invigorating confidence of our best traditions. One further consideration should not be suppressed. It would disregard the Judge's ironic spirit not to reflect, though lightheartedly, on the inimical or idolatrous feelings he would have stirred in those whose chief concern with Supreme Court decisions is the result and not, as it was for him, the nature and scope of the judicial process eventuating in decision, had he, as he certainly would have, applied on the Supreme Court the outlook governing adjudication that he expressed in the *Dennis* case (183 F. 2d 201) and in his Holmes Lectures. In any event it is a fact that in his later years he was not only reconciled to have missed the place natural for him but came to believe that the Fates were wiser in their disposition of him than he at one time desired for himself. Be this as it may, one thing is indubitably clear. Learned Hand's career vindicates a standard of excellence applied in performance that evokes universal esteem unconfused by show of place.

The individual contribution of judges is absorbed in the anonymity of the coral reef by which the judicial process shapes law. Their name and fame are writ in water. In the course of a century, the acclaim of a bare handful survives their day. Learned Hand now joins this most select company.

Meager is the survival value of judges even within the legal profession, and writers on *Kulturgeschichte* hardly take note of them. Rarest of all is the judge whose utterances serve as moral guides for his time. Less than a handful of the thousand judges who have occupied high judicial office during this century achieved this significance. Learned Hand was one of them, and by the time he reached old age he had become a legendary figure of wisdom. One can fix a specific date to the origin of this role, after he had been a judge for thirty-six years and had established his judicial preeminence but was hardly known outside his profession. By a single brief utterance of about five hundred words, spoken on May 21, 1944, in administering the oath to new citizens in Central Park, New York City, he leapt into popular acclaim and he sustained this position until his death, sixteen years later.

The occasion, on an I-Am-An-American Day, was front page news, and the main addresses, by a leading Senator and an eminent divine, received full reportage. Their utterances gather dust with the newspapers of the day in which

Judge Hand's presence was noted as the administrator of the oath, but not a word of his now famous utterance ("The Spirit of Liberty"). A few weeks later a writer, who happened to hear the speech over the radio and, hearing it, caught its significance, started the speech on its road to permanence by a piece in *The New Yorker*.

Judge Hand's contributions as a judge in the extensive fields of adjudication that came before him for more than fifty years, in those busy federal courts sitting in New York City, will form an important part of the body of American law during the twentieth century. Different aspects of his work were dealt with by specialists in the February issue of the *Harvard Law Review* (60 Harv. L. Rev. 325, *et seq.*) in celebration of his seventy-fifth birthday. Future studies will enlarge and sharpen these critical essays. But even those opinions of Judge Hand's vast output which disclose freshness of thought and fruitful insight are subject to the mortality of all judicial labor, barring only few doctrines of public law, like those associated with the name of Chief Justice Marshall, that will endure as long as the political framework survives of which they form a part. But Learned Hand's wisdom as a commentator on life are expressed in speeches and essays that will be enshrined in anthologies of English prose.

«« XXX »»

Prime Minister David Ben-Gurion

Mr. Justice Frankfurter helped take note of Prime Minister David Ben-Gurion's diamond jubilee in February 1962 with the following remarks in *The Jewish Frontier.*

HERZL imaginatively conceived Israel, Weizmann politically begat the state, Ben-Gurion brought it to full life. Such a broad generalization is unfair to their collaborators, especially to all the anonymous participants in their achievements. As Israel is not just another state, so Ben-Gurion is not just another Prime Minister. Israel has imposed its uniqueness on Ben-Gurion and Ben-Gurion has imposed his uniqueness on Israel. The war that gave it birth and the peace by which it must live, the diversified unity and the unifying diversity of its population, the miracle of its economic vitality that depends on the systematic pursuit of man's reasoned endeavors—all these and more are the exactions of Ben-Gurion's statemanship, as the variegated aspects of his own mind and character are reflected in the history of the state. As we hail him in full vitality on his seventy-fifth birthday, we have high hopes that he will be granted years long enough to enable him and his people to vindicate the moral claims of Israel in subduing even the most disturbing and most recalcitrant of the problems of Israel—reconciliation with its neighbors.

XXXI

Robert Frost

Mr. Justice Frankfurter was one of the speakers at a dinner on the occasion of the eighty-eighth birthday of Robert Frost. The dinner was held at the Pan-American Union on March 26, 1962. After some introductory words, in the course of which he set out the circumstances under which Robert Frost and he had become friends some forty years earlier, the Justice proceeded as follows:

Robert Frost is a moralist who does not moralize but instills. He is an educator who does not teach but shares. He makes us aware of what we so often look at but do not see. He makes us reflect on essentials by sidetracking trivia that preoccupy us. And Robert Frost does all this not by seducing us from actuality, nor awing us into insignificance. R. F. is deep but not abstruse. Nothing about him is soft or gnarled. We are not drawn to him either as escape or protest literature. He liberates; he liberates us from the episodic and the tawdry. But he does not shrink from the exactions and the inevitably tragic aspects of the human situation. In speaking tenderly of a friend who bravely attempted a profound tragic theme, Robert Frost said, "He's handicapped in doing so, for he has not suffered enough." Robert Frost confronts life. Nay, he manifests it. He is a poet not of passion but of compassion. Lincoln would have delighted in him and been comforted by him, as we are.

For his themes are eternal. Plato, Isaiah, Amos, Christ, Paul—all dealt with them. How often Robert Frost's poems are variations on the theme of wise humility. In diverse forms and through many hints and homespun verses he echoes Paul's admonition to the Corinthians: "If any man among you seemeth to be wise in this world, let him become a fool that he may be wise."

Automation creates problems for the economist, the social engineer, the statesman, and will create more. Perhaps, however, the most significant lesson that Colonel Glenn has taught us is that the most refined and most reliable of man's mechanical devisings sooner or later will fail and man is thrown back on man. Automation may displace the workman. It won't displace man on earth. Only man's folly can do it. And the poet as much as anyone may save us from that fate. What would the history of man have been without him? And the magic by which he saves us is as mysterious to him as it is to us. But there is no mystery about the fact that for civilization his role is indispensable and pervasive.

What that role is has been put in exalted terms, but not too exalted, by one of Robert Frost's immortal precursors.

> . . . The most unfailing herald, companion, and follower of the awakening of a great people to work a beneficial change in opinion or institution, is poetry. At such periods there is an accumulation of the power of communicating and receiving intense and impassioned conceptions respecting man and nature. The persons in whom this power resides, may often, as far as regards many portions of their nature, have little apparent correspondence with that spirit of good of which they are the ministers. But even whilst they deny and abjure, they are yet compelled to serve, the power which is seated on the throne of their own soul. It is impossible to read the compositions of the most celebrated writers of the present day without being startled with the electric life which burns within their words. They measure the circumference and sound the depths of human nature with a comprehensive and all-penetrating spirit, and they are themselves perhaps the most sincerely astonished at its manifestations; for it is less their spirit than the

spirit of the age. Poets are the hierophants of an unapprehended inspiration; the mirrors of the gigantic shadows which futurity casts upon the present; the words which express what they understand not; the trumpets which sing to battle, and feel not what they inspire; the influence which is moved not, but moves. Poets are the unacknowledged legislators of the world.[1]

[1] Percy Bysshe Shelley, *Defence of Poetry*, H. F. B. Brett-Smith, ed., in The Percy Reprints, No. 3 (Oxford, 1929).

⁂ XXXII ⁂

The Interstate Commerce Commission

On the morning of April 5, 1962, Mr. Justice Frankfurter attended the opening exercises in observance of the seventy-fifth anniversary of the Interstate Commerce Commission at the Department of Commerce Auditorium. As usual, he delivered his remarks without text or notes (later printed in House Doc. 492, 87th Cong. 2d Sess.). That afternoon, in his chambers at the Supreme Court, he was stricken with the illness that shortly resulted in his retirement from the Court.

MR. CHAIRMAN, past and present members of the Commission, ladies and gentlemen, celebration of a birthday of a long and worthy life is such an engaging and delightful event that when your Chairman asked me to take part in it, I thoughtlessly said I would be glad to do so. But being a questioning creature, I began to ask myself why I should have been asked. In the first place, I want to say that it is very generous of the Commission to invite me to take part in this event, because, while for twenty-three years as a teacher of law I lectured about the Commission, during the last twenty-three years from time to time I have dared to lecture to the Commission. Being an independent body, it has, I need not tell you, paid very little attention to my lectures.

Now, why are we here this morning? What are we celebrating? Duration is something; a long life is something; to live is something. You remember the Frenchman who when asked what he did during the French Revolution, proudly replied, "I survived."

Duration is something, but it isn't enough.

Why are we celebrating the Commission's seventy-fifth anniversary? Let me give a few reasons.

As your chairman has just indicated, one justification for my being here is that my life has almost been coterminous with the life of the Commission. I have lived through practically the whole of the effective existence of the Commission. I began life, professionally speaking, while the Elkins Act was in process of being born. And my first professional years, indeed the formative years of my professional life, were preoccupied with the indispensable aspects of the Interstate Commerce Act, its criminal sanctions, rebate provisions, et cetera. My first few years at the bar were devoted largely to such concerns. And, ever since, the life and activities of the Commission have continued to be one of my predominant concerns. I am here, as the chairman in his very polite and charmingly southern way indicated, as an exhibit of longevity.

What are we celebrating? I will give you four or five reasons, and I could give you many more, why today is an important event in the history of this country, in the history of the effective government of our society.

In the first place, the Commission illustrates, throughout its life, unblemished character. I would have supposed that one ought to take that—unblemished character—for granted. I don't merely mean character in the crude sense of the word, but character in its largest, affirmative sense—character meaning a fastidious regard for responsibility, a complete divorcement between public and private interest, and all the other concomitants of a true and worthy conception of public duty. Alas, that cannot be said of all public bodies, but it can be said that this Commission throughout its seventy-five years has had a career of unblemished character.

Secondly, I would say we are here to celebrate as striking a manifestation of competence in government as any I know of in the three branches of government. With all respect for each of those three branches, and I say this after having thought a good deal about it, my deep conviction is that, so far as competence with reference to the responsibilities which from 1887 to this day have been invested in it, this Commission has as high a record of competence as any element of the other three branches of the government with reference to its responsibilities.

As Congressman Harris has just indicated, competence isn't something abstract. Institutions may be more than the sum of their individual members, but institutions consist of human beings. And as Congressman Harris has observed, those who have performed the tantalizing, the difficult, and arduous tasks with which this body was charged from the beginning, have been, to a conspicuous degree, men of commanding ability.

Congressman Harris has mentioned some of them. It will not bore you too much, I hope, if I repeat that with the appointment of the first chairman, Judge Thomas M. Cooley—one of the greatest judges in the history of the United States, one of the great legal authors, one of the finest and most influential thinkers in the law—the Commission started out with a fine tradition. And it isn't like the sign that was posted in a backwater college to the effect that the traditions of this college are going into effect at 2:30 this afternoon. Traditions don't go into effect through notices. Traditions are created through men.

To start with a man like Cooley as chairman gave the Commission a great beginning. Congressman Harris has mentioned other names, but he has left out some that I would like to add. One of the most distinguished names, I think, on the roster of Commissioners is Franklin K. Lane. He exemplifies what I mean by saying that the qualities of Commissioners have not been inferior to the qualities of those in the other departments of the government. Franklin K. Lane, I happen to know, was very seriously considered for a place on the supreme bench of this country, and it is not mere fantasy to say that if he had not been Canadian by birth, he might well have been considered as a candidate for the Presidency. Others deserving mention along with Lane are Commissioner Clements and Chairman Knapp, who thereafter became a circuit judge of the United States after he had been presiding judge at the commerce court. And then there are two distinguished nonlawyers, Commissioner Meyer and Professor Daniels, of Princeton, who are outstanding in a field in which most men come from the law—a matter not of partiality, but, I think, relevance, because, on the whole, the matters that come before the Commission closely concern, if not the subject matter of lawyers, at least their mode of dealing with problems.

I could go on with others, mentioning only those that have gone beyond, telling you of these men of high competence, and of the conditions that clearly must be present for competence to become effective. Congressman Harris has said he thought it was good policy to have continuity. If he will allow me to say so, I don't think it is merely good policy, I think it is absolutely necessary policy for an institution like the Interstate Commerce Commission to have continuity of service. And speaking of that, Mr. Chairman, it deserves to be mentioned that during the first fifty years of the existence of your Commission, you had only three secretaries, and one of them, Edward A. Moseley, was not a secretary in the ordinary sense.

I wish it were compulsory for students in our high schools, or at least our colleges, and certainly for Commissioners, to read the biography of Joseph B. Eastman, by Dr. Claude Fuess, and also James Morgan's biography of Edward A. Moseley, the first secretary of the Commission, who was there from 1887 to something like 1911 or 1912. Moseley was not merely a secretary within the ordinary implications or connotations of that term. He was responsible, perhaps more than any one single man, for the enactment of the Safety Appliance Act and the Federal Employers Liability Act.

For fifty years there were only three secretaries carrying on all those important and largely anonymous functions of secretary. These are the officials to whom monuments are not erected, but who are really the driving force of our governmental machinery. That is why I say continuity is not merely a good policy but an essential policy.

Thirdly, it is a necessary condition, before a Commission can effectively act, that it be independent. I do not mean independent because the statute says it shall be independent, or because speeches are made about being independent, or because the President says it is expected to be independent, but because Commissioners actively assert independence when the occasion calls for independence.

Let me give you an illustration. Chairman Eastman was a vigorous personality. In the late twenties, Commissioner Eastman, as he then was, encountered another vigorous personality, the then Secretary of Commerce, Mr. Herbert Hoover. Not only was Secretary Hoover vigorous, but he had a very considerable grasp of economic problems and a belief in his reach, sometimes extending beyond his grasp. He realized that railroad tariffs and rate regulation have a considerable influence upon the economic life of the nation.

The Commission had before it for consideration the matter of transcontinental rate structures. Secretary Hoover had strong views on that subject and he communicated those views with some vigor to Commissioner Eastman. Mr. Eastman indicated to the Secretary of Commerce that that was none of his business. I speak with the bluntness with which Eastman used to speak. And those two dedicated public servants clashed in a gentlemanly way as to their respective spheres of authority.

Eastman, needless to say, was right. The Commission must determine rate structures, demands for increased rates, or demands for lowering of rates, on the proceedings that go on before it, and not by reference to the views— no matter how highly informed, no matter how highly placed —of an outsider.

In due course, Secretary Hoover became President Hoover, and termination of Eastman's tenure also happened, unfortunately, to coincide with the first year of Hoover's Presidency. And, in perfect good faith, President Hoover thought that Eastman wasn't a good man to continue as an Interstate Commerce Commissioner, a perfectly natural conclusion. It requires angels to think well of people who resist their powers.

Eastman did nothing about his reappointment—nothing. That is the kind of person he was. But the whole New England delegation in Congress vigorously urged the reappointment of Commissioner Eastman. All the New England roads who had the most intimate knowledge of Eastman—he had previously been utility commissioner in Massachusetts—petitioned the President, urging him to reappoint Eastman. In their memorial they set forth that they disagreed with Eastman's general outlook and they often suffered, from his hands, decisions and views contrary to their private interest. But Eastman, they said, was a wholly disinterested, highly competent public servant, and the public interest, transcending differences of views, transcending differences of relationships, transcending clashes of personality, demanded that Eastman be reappointed.

He was reappointed, and in that episode, I think, is the key to what an independent agency needs. Independence cannot be conferred on one: it must be exercised. And so it was that Eastman was appointed first by President Wilson; he was reappointed by Harding; he was reappointed by Hoover; he was reappointed by Roosevelt. And there is the key to all this, what shall I say, rhetorical talk about an independent agency. Independence must be asserted: it cannot be conferred; it cannot be granted.

So I regard continuity in office and an active assertion of independence, by those who are charged with the responsibility of independence, as the essential conditions under which a commission like the Interstate Commerce Commission must function, and, as a matter of history, has functioned.

Fourthly, I would suggest that the Interstate Commerce Commission is a good laboratory for the solving of governmental problems in the domain of economics. It was a touchingly naïve, perhaps romantic, President of the United States, who said that government, after all, is a very simple thing. What was simple was not government, but he. The tragedy of his life was that he learned about that too late, having spent his life before he became President in talking and writing. He discovered too late the difference between having responsibility for acting and merely talking and writing.

Now, the Interstate Commerce Commission illustrates, strikingly, I think, how this country has dealt with its basic economic problems—not dogmatically, but pragmatically, empirically, by trial and error, distrusting all absolutes, whether of private enterprise or government control. The fact of the matter is that throughout our history—and when I say "throughout our history," I go back to the Colonies—we have had a mixed economy in this country, not merely private enterprise free from all governmental intervention or control, not absorbing governmental control, but a mixture, and a mixture in varying proportions at different times. It makes all the difference whether you have a dogmatic view about these problems, an either/or view—private enterprise without control, or control without private enterprise—or you respond to the complexities of life by evolving complex solutions to its problems.

Congressman Harris has sketched for you the history of the Interstate Commerce Act's coming into being. Chief Justice Hughes rightly said that if it had come into being earlier we would have been saved many troubles later. But the fact is that the Interstate Commerce Act illustrates a blend of preserving, furthering, and encouraging private incentive, with due regard for effective, informed representation of the public interest where, as in all aspects of transportation, private enterprise closely touches the national well-being.

The upshot has been a succession of enactments beginning with the tentative start in 1887, the restrictive interpretations of the act through the decisions of the Supreme Court of the United States, the amendment of the Elkins Act in 1903, the Hepburn Act in 1906, and the Mann-Elkins Act in 1910, and so on down to the Transportation Act of 1940 which now governs the transportation system of the United States. This process, this empirical advance in legislative oversight and enactment, is a response—a response to the actualities of life.

It was John Stuart Mill, I think, who said that progress consists of bringing opinions in conformity to fact. But if you look at facts through the colored glasses of your own opinion, you aren't going to make very much progress. So you have the legislative clashes in successive enactments—the pipeline amendments, the commodity clause, and so on. Those clashes in the legislature, if I may be permitted a generalization, were due not so much, as some writers easily assumed, to selfishness in outlook or different local considerations as to a disregard of the dictum of Mill to bring opinion in conformity with fact. And one by one these measures encountered, not narrow-minded people, but people who had not yet brought their opinions in conformity with the changing character of the economic forces of our society.

I am bound to say that in my regard the leading lawyer of his day, William Evarts—as distinguished a lawyer as there is in our history, but an old gentleman at that time—thought the world would come to an end if the Interstate Commerce Act was passed, because it violated his notions of the separation of powers and judicial review, and all the rest. So the Interstate Commerce Commission, in enforcing the Interstate Commerce Act, illustrates that these complicated questions cannot be determined by slogans—separation of powers, nondelegation of legislative power, due process of law, et cetera, et cetera. There must be a defined, particularized analysis of the economic situation in relation to the restrictions upon the power, both of Congress and the President, and everybody else under our Constitution, subject also to the limitations which the Supreme Court, from time to time at least, recognizes as to its own powers.

I have pointed to the fact that this Commission has had an unblemished character, has been manned on the whole by men of high competence, including not merely the picture-card Commissioners but its unknown secretaries, and its legal counsel, and its still larger staff of examiners.

(Some of the ablest lawyers I have ever known started in life as examiners of the Interstate Commerce Commission.) It has maintained not merely formal independence, but actual independence of word and deed, and has been a laboratory demonstration of how economic problems may be worked out by trial and error. Finally, by virtue of all these considerations, the Commission has been a pacemaker, a model, for the subsequent commissions which, in turn, have been created in response to economic and social demands in their fields of activity. Of course, no institution gives a model carbon copy for an institution in other fields of government. But, on the whole, all the other commissions have, in their procedures, in their directions, in their outlook, in their ways of doing business, been modeled, at least as to the starting points for legislative formulation and administrative action, after the Interstate Commerce Commission.

This Commission, like every other commission, lives in the conviction of the totality of government, and it lives beyond that in the context of our whole people. It derives its power through the Congress of the United States. Figuratively speaking, I think it is fair to say, so well has this Commission conducted its life, that it has been a continuous standing committee of advice to the Congress of the United States as to proposals for needed amendatory legislation. Not only that, it has, of course, operated in close relation to the courts. And, in this connection, it makes a great deal of difference how the Commission behaves, what kinds of records it prepares, what kinds of procedures it devises; all those things largely determine the extent to which judicial review will leave its rulings unscathed.

Finally, there is the public. I hope it is not merely an old man's concern that leads me to say that too often people think that publicity is a policy. Rather, publicity is the product of policy, and the sort of publicity generated depends on whether the policy is good or bad. I do not think the Interstate Commerce Commission has either anticipated or followed Madison Avenue as one of its chief concerns. The image, to use that awful, modern term which preoccupies the press but ought not to preoccupy the public, which it has created for itself in the eyes of the railroads, the water carriers, the truck concerns, and particularly the lawyers who serve those interests has been due to the intrinsic quality of its performance and not to any publicity effort.

One word more and I am done. It is a very wise man who said that institutions do not die, they commit suicide. And you can commit suicide by just ceasing to have life. I hope, and I have the highest confidence, that the Interstate Commerce Commission will remember the other part of that phrase of Ecclesiasticus, "Let us now praise famous men, and our fathers that begat us" and continue to live in the spirit of the great men who preceded them. Continue to live in their spirits with reference to your problems and seventy-five years from now there will be an even more appreciative audience and nation grateful to the Commission for its achievements.

XXXIII

Retirement From the Court

On August 28th, 1962, Mr. Justice Frankfurter submitted his letter of retirement to President Kennedy. On September 28th, he wrote to his brethren on the Court in response to their letter expressing regret at his retirement. The exchange of letters between the Justice and the President and between the Justice and his brethren on the Court are set out below.

August 28, 1962

My dear Mr. President:

Pursuant to the provisions of 28 U.S.C. Section 371(b), 68 Stat. 12, I hereby retire at the close of this day from regular active service as an Associate Justice of the Supreme Court of the United States.

The occasion for my retirement arises from the affliction which I unexpectedly suffered last April. Since then I have undergone substantial improvement. High expectations were earlier expressed by my doctors that I would be able to resume my judicial duties with the beginning of the next Term of the Court, commencing October 1. However, they now advise me that the stepped-up therapy essential to that end involves hazards which might jeopardize the useful years they anticipate still lie ahead of me.

The Court should not enter its new Term with uncertainty as to whether I might later be able to return to unrestricted duty. To retain my seat on the basis of a

These two exchanges of letters may be found at 371 U.S. viii–xiii (1962).

diminished work schedule would not comport with my own philosophy or with the demands of the business of the Court. I am thus left with no choice but to regard my period of active service on the Court as having run its course.

I need hardly tell you, Mr. President, of the reluctance with which I leave the institution whose concerns have been the absorbing interest of my life. May I again convey to you my gratitude for your call upon me during the summer and for the solicitude you were kind enough to express.

With high respect and esteem,

Faithfully yours,
Felix Frankfurter

August 28, 1962

My dear Mr. Justice Frankfurter:

Your retirement from regular active service on the Supreme Court ends a long and illustrious chapter in your life, and I understand well how hard a choice you have made. Along with all your host of friends I have followed with admiration your gallant and determined recovery, and I have shared the general hope that you would return soon to the Court's labors. From my own visit I know of your undiminished spirit and your still contagious zest for life. That you now take the judgment of the doctors and set it sternly against your own demanding standard of judicial effectiveness is characteristic, but it comes as an immediate disappointment.

Still, if you allow it, I will say there is also consolation in your decision. I believe it good for you as well as for the rest of us that you should now be free, in reflective leisure, for activities that are impossible in the demanding life of Justice of the Supreme Court. You have been part of American public life for well over half a century. What you have learned of the meaning of our country is reflected, of course, in many hundreds of opinions, in thousands of your students, and in dozens of books and articles. But you have a great deal still to tell us, and therefore I am glad to know that the doctors are telling you, in effect, not to retire, but only to turn to a new line of work, with new promise of service to the nation.

Meanwhile, I should like to offer to Mrs. Frankfurter and to you, for myself and for all Americans, our respectful gratitude for the character, courage, learning and judicial dedication with which you have served your country over the last twenty-three years.

Sincerely,
John Kennedy

September 27, 1962

Dear Justice Frankfurter:

As the opening day of our 1962 Term approaches, it becomes increasingly difficult for all of us to realize that you will not be in your accustomed chair, which you filled with such distinction and in such good fellowship with your colleagues for almost a quarter of a century.

All of us, except Mr. Justice White, our newest member, have served with you for years and we, more than any others, will feel the loss that comes from your retirement. We regret the necessity for it, but we reluctantly accept your decision because your doctor has told you and us that if this course is pursued there will be opened to you new avenues of usefulness to the profession to which you dedicated yourself 60 years ago.

Every one of these years was an eventful year for you as you strained every fiber of your mind and body to the administration of justice and to the welfare of the Court. Few men in the life of the Supreme Court have made contributions to its jurisprudence equal to your own. As a scholar, teacher, critic, public servant, and a member of the Court for 24 Terms, you have woven your philosophy of law and your conception of our institutions into its annals where all may read them and profit thereby.

Your retirement does not end our association. It merely changes the form of it. You will always be one of us, and after rest and relaxation from the rigors of the Court work restore you to health, we look forward to years of continued happy association with you. In the meantime, our best wishes for a rapid recovery will always be with you.

Sincerely,
Earl Warren
Hugo L. Black
Wm. O. Douglas
Tom C. Clark
John M. Harlan
Wm. J. Brennan, Jr.
Potter Stewart
Byron R. White

September 28, 1962

My dear Brethren:

It would be unnatural for me not to address you thus, although you have been apprised that I have advised the President of my decision to retire as of August 28th, under the appropriate provisions of law, as an active member of the Court. I still address you as I do, for the endeavors which the business of the Court entails in the daily intimacy of our association have forged bonds of fellowship which cannot be abruptly severed. The final manifestation of your fraternal feelings toward me, your letter of September 27th, your generous words of farewell, are a cheering close to our uniformly happy curial relations over the years, and I shall enduringly cherish your moving letter. Retiring from active membership on the Court of itself would involve a wrench in my life, but the fact is that I have served the Court in one professional way or another almost from the day I ceased to be a law student, not merely during the years I have actually been on the bench.

My years on the Court have only deepened my conviction that its existence and functioning according to its best historic traditions are indispensable for the well-being of the nation. The nature of the issues which are involved in the legal controversies that are inevitable under our constitutional system does not warrant the nation to expect identity of views among the members of the Court regarding such issues, nor even agreement on the routes of thought by which decisions are reached. The nation is merely warranted in expecting harmony of aims among those who have been called to the Court. This means pertinacious pursuit of the processes of reason in the disposition of controversies that come before the Court. This presupposes intellectual disinterestedness in the analysis of the factors involved in the issues that call for decision. This in turn requires rigorous self-scrutiny to discover, with a view to curbing, every influence that may deflect from such disinterestedness.

I have spent many happy years in fellowship with you and I carry away the abiding memory of years of comradeship grappling with problems worthy of the best in fallible men.

My best wishes for happy, long years for each of you and continued satisfying labors, and every good wish that the Court may continue its indispensable role in the evolution of our beloved nation.

With the happiest memories, I am,

Sincerely and faithfully yours,
Felix Frankfurter

XXXIV

Niels Bohr

Niels Bohr, Nobel Laureate in Physics in 1922, was an important member of the Los Alamos team that worked out the beginnings of the atomic era. He left Denmark, his native land, to come to this country during the war only after exhausting his possibilities of protecting the victims of Nazi persecution. He returned to Denmark in 1945 and subsequently became head of that country's atomic energy commission. In 1957 he was awarded the first Atoms for Peace Prize. The following letter was written by Mr. Justice Frankfurter to *The New York Times* on November 27, 1962 and was published under the heading: "Justice Frankfurter Pays Tribute to Friend of Many Years."

WITH MY profound ignorance of science, including the history of science, it would be impertinent of me even to join the chorus of adulation of Niels Bohr as the great scientist, but thanks to the privilege of having enjoyed a rather close friendship with him over the years, I think I am in a position to say that however great a scientist he was, he was even a rarer phenomenon as a noble character.

When the history of the Resistance movement in Denmark will be fully recorded, Niels Bohr's individual efforts, with the Damocles' sword of death hanging over him himself, in giving refuge and helping with the liberation of many fellow victims, will form a notable chapter.

And one can confidently say that on no conscience did the potential menace of nuclear physics to mankind weigh more heavily than it did on Professor Bohr. Equally, I believe, is it true that no man was so preoccupied with thinking about means of alleviation of this menace than the persistent thought that Professor Bohr gave to this aspect of the matter.

I hope it is not impertinent for me to say that one aspect of his scientific significance has not been adequately accentuated, for it was not only by his personal contributions that he made himself, as those who are competent to judge assess him, one of the greatest scientists of the century. He was not only a personal contributor, but many important scientists came to him in his Copenhagen Institute from all over the world to draw on his wisdom and learning, and, beyond that, in many instances he became the *accoucheur* of their brain children.

XXXV

Lord Brand

In still another *Nachruf*—the term is the Justice's—to a frequent English visitor to these shores, Mr. Justice Frankfurter, in a letter to *The Times* (London), September 16, 1963, mourns the passing of his friend Lord Brand. Brand was a distinguished economist, one-time president of the Royal Economic Society and Fellow of All Souls College, Oxford, who spent the greater portion of his career in government service. Among the posts he held that caused his path to cross and recross that of Mr. Justice Frankfurter was that of financial adviser to Lord Robert Cecil at the Paris Peace Conference in 1919, deputy chairman of the British mission to Washington in 1917–18, member of the British Food Mission in Washington in 1941–44, and representative of His Majesty's Treasury in Washington in 1944–46.

As one of his oldest American friends, I cannot forgo saying a few words, however inadequate, of farewell to Lord Brand, and I am confident that the sentiments which I shall express fairly reflect the feelings of his many other and diversified American friends.

It is very sad for all of us that we can no longer look forward to a visit from that gentle and wise man who gave all of us both pleasure and stimulus in the course of his intermittent visits to the United States, and since he, with characteristic generosity, discredited the cynical saying that "out of sight is out of mind," we shall not even have from time to time the thoughtful and stimulating letters in the course of which he discussed world affairs, particularly Anglo-American relations. He was one of the strongest supporters of the view, if I may echo Sir Winston Churchill, that companionship in thought and action between the United Kingdom and the United States is indispensable for the peace of the world. And he also kept us, his friends, abreast of what was going on throughout the British Commonwealth by making us, through his kindness, regular recipients of the *Round Table*, of which he was, I believe, one of the founders and for all I know one of its editors and certainly one its controlling forces.

It was characteristic of Brand that the last visit I had from him was in a hospital, when he learnt that I had been invalided. At the time, the international sky was dark and threatening, but he early perceived the interdependence of economic and political problems beyond conventional national boundaries. He saw that problems that on the surface had seemingly only national aspects had in fact more significantly international aspects for Europe as an entirety and indeed were so interdependent for the world as a whole that they also significantly affected the United States. As he left me, I felt as I always did when he left me, not only cheered but enlightened.

Bob Brand was one of the sweetest natures it was my good fortune ever to encounter, but with his sweetness there was a deep vein of steel in his make-up, and it was this which enabled him to absorb with resilient fortitude the two cruel blows that fate meted out to him. The first was the death of his beautiful wife, Phyllis, and the second, the death as the second World War was drawing to a close of his only son, which in such circumstances he rightly called "a wasteful loss of life." While he was especially attached to his son, he was no less devoted to his two daughters, who happily inherited their mother's charm and thereby doubtless reminded him from time to time that his life's helpmate was no longer by his side. For Phyllis Langhorne was as lovely a creature as she was beautiful in presence and uniquely fitted to be his wife.

I am confident that when the archives are opened, along with the relevant private papers relating to the Lothian and Halifax missions, it will be found that Brand was an important and wise counsellor of both of those ambassadors. As for the American story concerning Lord Brand's role during the Halifax and Lothian ambassadorships, it is safe to predict that when that is revealed through the biographies and autobiographies of leading American figures of that time he will be seen to have been an equally welcome and valued adviser to them. Not one of the so-called private and unofficial ambassadors active in promoting harmonious Anglo-American relations was more effective or more welcome than Lord Brand was in his quiet way.

XXXVI

John Henry Wigmore

Dean Wigmore was one of the leading spirits of the law school world throughout his long tenure as Dean of the Northwestern University Law School. He was a seminal scholar, a magisterial administrator, and an aggressive personality. In spite of essential differences of view between them, Mr. Justice Frankfurter maintained the highest respect for Wigmore's scholarly capacities and readily responded to a request that he contribute to the *Northwestern University Law Review*'s commemoration of the centennial of Wigmore's birth in 1963 (58:443 [September-October 1963]).

John Henry Wigmore contributed to the consciousness of the law. He not only added substantially to its literature in many ways—he changed the climate of opinion in which judges and lawyers have since his time, and through him, carried on their functions in the law.

Wigmore's *Treatise on Evidence* is unrivaled as the greatest treatise on any single subject of the law. I make no exception to this superlative statement. It is not only a great treatise on the law of evidence, but it is a masterpiece of scholarship, conveyed through a distinguished style of writing. He has, of course, been of inestimable value to every judge and every lawyer who has had to deal with any problem in the law of evidence. I would make his treatise compulsory reading in every university that has the ambition to turn out its graduates as competent masters of the English language, not merely for the original parts written by Wigmore himself but for the marvelous collection of otherwise unavailable quotations.

But Wigmore's contribution to the law was not limited to one field. For instance, he was one of the founders, with Holmes, of the whole changed outlook of our law in what we now call torts. I am honored to pay tribute to that great man's contribution to the law on the centennial of his birth.

Atheneum Paperbacks

HISTORY

3 SIX MEDIEVAL MEN AND WOMEN *by H. S. Bennett*
10 TRAVEL AND DISCOVERY IN THE RENAISSANCE *by Boies Penrose*
30 GHANA IN TRANSITION *by David E. Apter*
58 TROTSKY'S DIARY IN EXILE—1935 *translated by Elena Zarudnaya*
63 THE SINO-SOVIET CONFLICT 1956–1961 *by Donald S. Zagoria*
65 LORD AND PEASANT IN RUSSIA FROM THE NINTH TO THE NINETEENTH CENTURY *by Jerome Blum*
68 TWELVE WHO RULED *by Robert R. Palmer*
83 KARAMZIN'S MEMOIR ON ANCIENT AND MODERN RUSSIA *by Richard Pipes*
97 THE EIGHTEENTH CENTURY CONFRONTS THE GODS *by Frank E. Manuel*
103 JACOBEAN PAGEANT *by G. P. V. Akrigg*
104 THE MAKING OF VICTORIAN ENGLAND *by G. Kitson Clark*
107 RUSSIA LEAVES THE WAR *by George F. Kennan*
108 THE DECISION TO INTERVENE *by George F. Kennan*
121 DRIVING FORCES IN HISTORY *by Halvdan Koht*
124 THE FORMATION OF THE SOVIET UNION *by Richard Pipes*
127 THE THREE LIVES OF CHARLES DE GAULLE *by David Schoenbrun*
128 AS FRANCE GOES *by David Schoenbrun*
141 SERGEI WITTE AND THE INDUSTRIALIZATION OF RUSSIA *by Theodore Von Laue*

HISTORY–ASIA

44 CHINA'S RESPONSE TO THE WEST *by Ssu-Yü Teng and John K. Fairbank*
63 THE SINO-SOVIET CONFLICT 1956–1961 *by Donald S. Zagoria*
64 CONFUCIANISM AND CHINESE CIVILIZATION *edited by Arthur F. Wright*
70 THE CHINA TANGLE *by Herbert Feis*
77 BUDDHISM IN CHINESE HISTORY *by Arthur F. Wright*
87 A DOCUMENTARY HISTORY OF CHINESE COMMUNISM *by Conrad Brandt, Benjamin Schwartz and John K. Fairbank*
92 THE LAST STAND OF CHINESE CONSERVATISM *by Mary Clabaugh Wright*
93 THE TRAGEDY OF THE CHINESE REVOLUTION *by Harold R. Isaacs*
94 THE AGRARIAN ORIGINS OF MODERN JAPAN *by Thomas C. Smith*

THE NEW YORK TIMES BYLINE BOOKS

CHINA *by Harry Schwartz*
RUSSIA *by Harrison E. Salisbury*
THE MIDDLE EAST *by Jay Walz*
AFRICA *by Waldemar A. Nielsen*
LATIN AMERICA *by Tad Szulc*
SOUTHEAST ASIA *by Tillman Durdin*

Atheneum Paperbacks

STUDIES IN AMERICAN NEGRO LIFE

NL1 THE NEGRO IN COLONIAL NEW ENGLAND *by Lorenzo Johnston Greene*
NL2 SEPARATE AND UNEQUAL *by Louis R. Harlan*
NL3 AFTER FREEDOM *by Hortense Powdermaker*
NL4 FREDERICK DOUGLASS *by Benjamin Quarles*
NL5 PREFACE TO PEASANTRY *by Arthur F. Raper*
NL6 W.E.B. DU BOIS: PROPAGANDIST OF THE NEGRO PROTEST *by Elliott Rudwick*
NL7 THE BLACK WORKER *by Sterling D. Spero and Abram L. Harris*
NL8 A&B THE MAKING OF BLACK AMERICA *edited by August Meier and Elliott Rudwick, 2 vols.*
NL9 BLACK MANHATTAN *by James Weldon Johnson*
NL10 THE NEW NEGRO *edited by Alain Locke*
NL11 THE NEGRO'S GOD AS REFLECTED IN HIS LITERATURE *by Benjamin Mays*
NL12 NEGRO POETRY AND DRAMA AND THE NEGRO IN AMERICAN FICTION *by Sterling Brown*
NL13 WHEN NEGROES MARCH *by Herbert Garfinkel*
NL14 PHILOSOPHY AND OPINIONS OF MARCUS GARVEY *by Marcus Garvey, edited by Amy Jacques-Garvey*
NL15 FREE NEGRO LABOR AND PROPERTY IN ANTE-BELLUM VIRGINIA *by Luther Jackson*
NL17 SEA ISLAND TO CITY *by Clyde Vernon Kiser*
NL18 NEGRO EDUCATION IN ALABAMA *by Horace Mann Bond*

LAW AND GOVERNMENT

20 A&B DOCUMENTS ON FUNDAMENTAL HUMAN RIGHTS *edited by Zechariah Chafee, Jr., 2 vols.*
23 THE CONSTITUTION AND WHAT IT MEANS TODAY *by Edward S. Corwin*
27 COURTS ON TRIAL *by Jerome Frank*
30 GHANA IN TRANSITION *by David E. Apter*
46 THE FUTURE OF FEDERALISM *by Nelson A. Rockefeller*
53 THE BILL OF RIGHTS *by Learned Hand*
72 MR. JUSTICE HOLMES AND THE SUPREME COURT *by Felix Frankfurter*
73 THE STRUCTURE OF FREEDOM *by Christian Bay*
84 THE DIMENSIONS OF LIBERTY *by Oscar and Mary Handlin*
89 MAKERS OF MODERN STRATEGY *edited by Edward M. Earle*
105 DILEMMAS OF URBAN AMERICA *by Robert C. Weaver*
110 DRED SCOTT'S CASE *by Vincent C. Hopkins, S.J.*
130 THE REVOLUTION OF THE SAINTS *by Michael Walzer*
138 OF LAW AND LIFE AND OTHER THINGS THAT MATTER *by Felix Frankfurter, edited by Philip B. Kurland*

Atheneum Paperbacks

DIPLOMACY AND INTERNATIONAL RELATIONS

2 POWER AND DIPLOMACY *by Dean Acheson*
4 THE ROAD TO PEARL HARBOR *by Herbert Feis*
15 CALL TO GREATNESS *by Adlai E. Stevenson*
34 THE DIPLOMACY OF ECONOMIC DEVELOPMENT *by Eugene B. Black*
40 THE UNITED STATES AND MEXICO *by Howard F. Cline*
41 THE DIPLOMATS 1919–1939 *by Gordon A. Craig and*
A&B *Felix Gilbert*
44 CHINA'S RESPONSE TO THE WEST *by Ssu-Yü Teng and John K. Fairbank*
54 STRATEGIC SURRENDER *by Paul Kecskemeti*
63 THE SINO-SOVIET CONFLICT 1956–1961 *by Donald S. Zagoria*
70 THE CHINA TANGLE *by Herbert Feis*
74 STALIN'S FOREIGN POLICY REAPPRAISED *by Marshall Shulman*
89 MAKERS OF MODERN STRATEGY *edited by Edward M. Earle*
107 RUSSIA LEAVES THE WAR *by George F. Kennan*
108 THE DECISION TO INTERVENE *by George F. Kennan*

ECONOMICS AND BUSINESS

21 BIG BUSINESS LEADERS IN AMERICA *by W. Lloyd Warner and James Abegglen*
24 PROSPERITY AND DEPRESSION *by Gottfried Haberler*
34 THE DIPLOMACY OF ECONOMIC DEVELOPMENT *by Eugene R. Black*
47 ECONOMIC CONCENTRATION AND THE MONOPOLY PROBLEM *by Edward S. Mason*
78 THE ECONOMICS OF DEFENSE IN THE NUCLEAR AGE *by Charles J. Hitch and Roland N. McKean*
80 FOUNDATIONS OF ECONOMIC ANALYSIS *by Paul Anthony Samuelson*
86 THE CORPORATION IN MODERN SOCIETY *edited by Edward S. Mason*

PSYCHOLOGY AND SOCIOLOGY

21 BIG BUSINESS LEADERS IN AMERICA *by W. Lloyd Warner and James Abegglen*
67 ON KNOWING *by Jerome S. Bruner*
79 THE SOCIETY OF CAPTIVES *by Gresham M. Sykes*
109 AFRICAN HOMICIDE AND SUICIDE *edited by Paul Bohannan*
119 THE LAW OF PRIMITIVE MAN *by E. Adamson Hoebel*
120 THE SOVIET CITIZEN *by Alex Inkeles and Raymond Bauer*
133 THE FAMILY REVOLUTION IN MODERN CHINA *by Marion J. Levy, Jr.*

Atheneum Paperbacks

THE WORLDS OF NATURE AND MAN

5 OF MEN AND MOUNTAINS *by William O. Douglas*
18 THE SUDDEN VIEW *by Sybille Bedford*
22 SPRING IN WASHINGTON *by Louis J. Halle*
33 LOST CITY OF THE INCAS *by Hiram Bingham*
45 THE SEA SHORE *by C. M. Yonge*
61 THE NEW YORK TIMES GUIDE TO DINING OUT IN NEW YORK *edited by Craig Claiborne*
81 THE NEW YORK TIMES GUIDE TO HOME FURNISHING *edited by Barbara Plumb and Elizabeth Sverbeyeff*
82 BIRDS AND MEN *by Robert H. Welker*
95 THE FIRMAMENT OF TIME *by Loren Eiseley*

LITERATURE AND THE ARTS

1 ROME AND A VILLA *by Eleanor Clark*
8 THE MUSICAL EXPERIENCE OF COMPOSER, PERFORMER, LISTENER *by Roger Sessions*
11 THE GRANDMOTHERS *by Glenway Wescott*
12 i: SIX NONLECTURES *by e. e. cummings*
14 THE PRESENCE OF GRACE *by J. F. Powers*
18 THE SUDDEN VIEW *by Sybille Bedford*
25 THE ROBBER BRIDEGROOM *by Eudora Welty*
29 CONTEXTS OF CRITICISM *by Harry Levin*
36 GEORGE BERNARD SHAW *by Hesketh Pearson*
37 THE TERRITORY AHEAD *by Wright Morris*
39 THE LETTERS OF VINCENT VAN GOGH *edited by Mark Roskill*
42 THE GREEN MARE *by Marcel Aymé*
50 AMERICAN ARCHITECTURE AND OTHER WRITINGS *by Montgomery Schuyer, edited by William H. Jordy and Ralph Coe; abridged by William H. Jordy*
55 PNIN *by Vladimir Nabokov*
66 SELECTED POEMS INCLUDING THE WOMAN AT THE WASHINGTON ZOO *by Randall Jarrell*
76 THE SINGER OF TALES *by Albert B. Lord*
90 ANATOMY OF CRITICISM *by Northrop Frye*
96 CONRAD THE NOVELIST *by Albert J. Guerard*
99 MARK TWAIN *by Henry Nash Smith*
102 EMILY DICKINSON *by Thomas H. Johnson*
112 THE LIFE OF THE DRAMA *by Eric Bentley*
114 SELECTED MARK TWAIN-HOWELLS LETTERS *edited by Frederick Anderson, William Gibson, and Henry Nash Smith*
122 REPORTING THE NEWS *edited by Louis M. Lyons*
131 WHAT IS THEATRE? (*incorporating* THE DRAMATIC EVENT) *by Eric Bentley*
135 THE HERO OF THE WAVERLY NOVELS *by Alexander Welsh*
143 POETS OF REALITY *by J. Hillis Miller*